JENS KLEIN BALLOONS

Spector Books

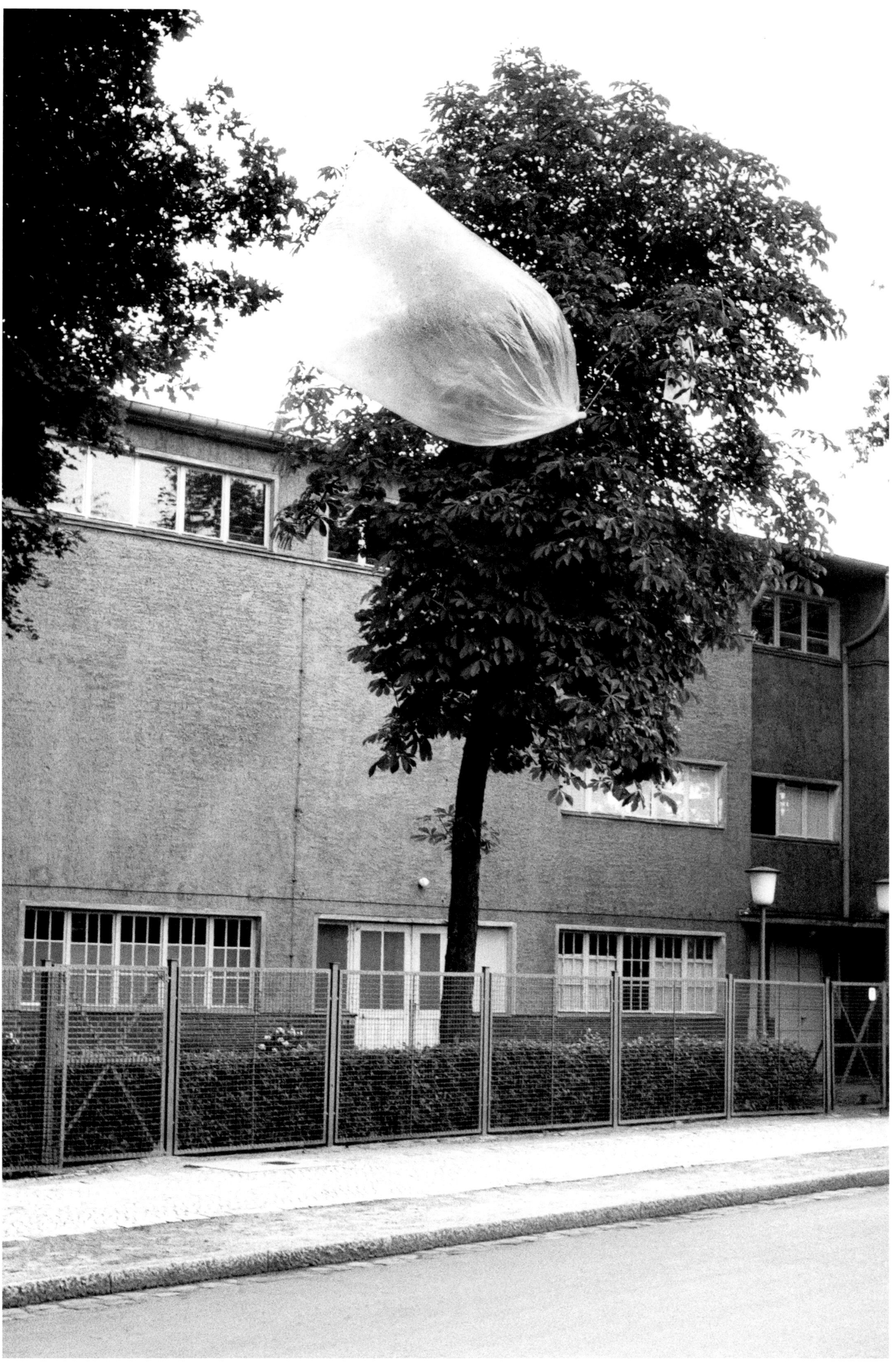

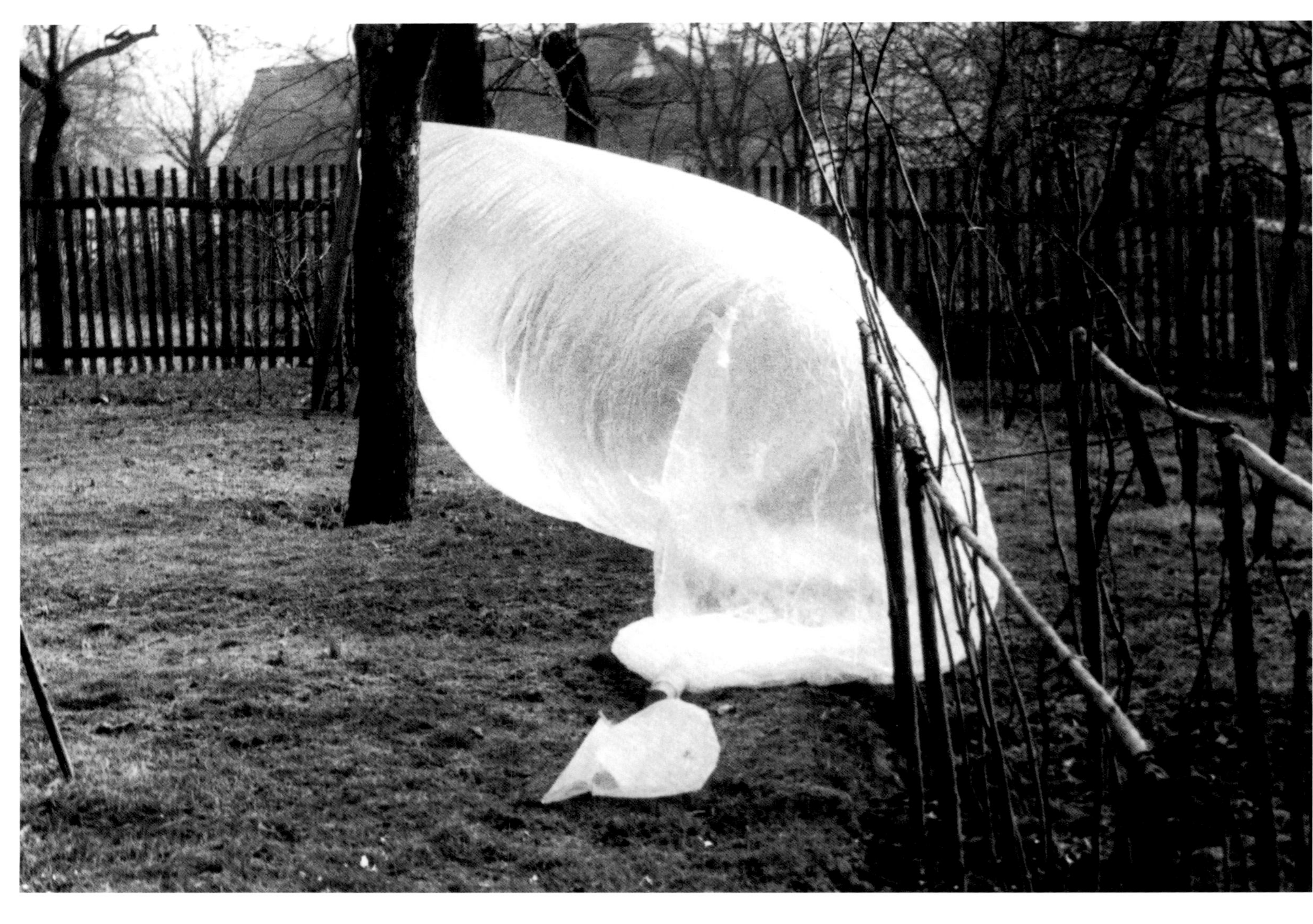

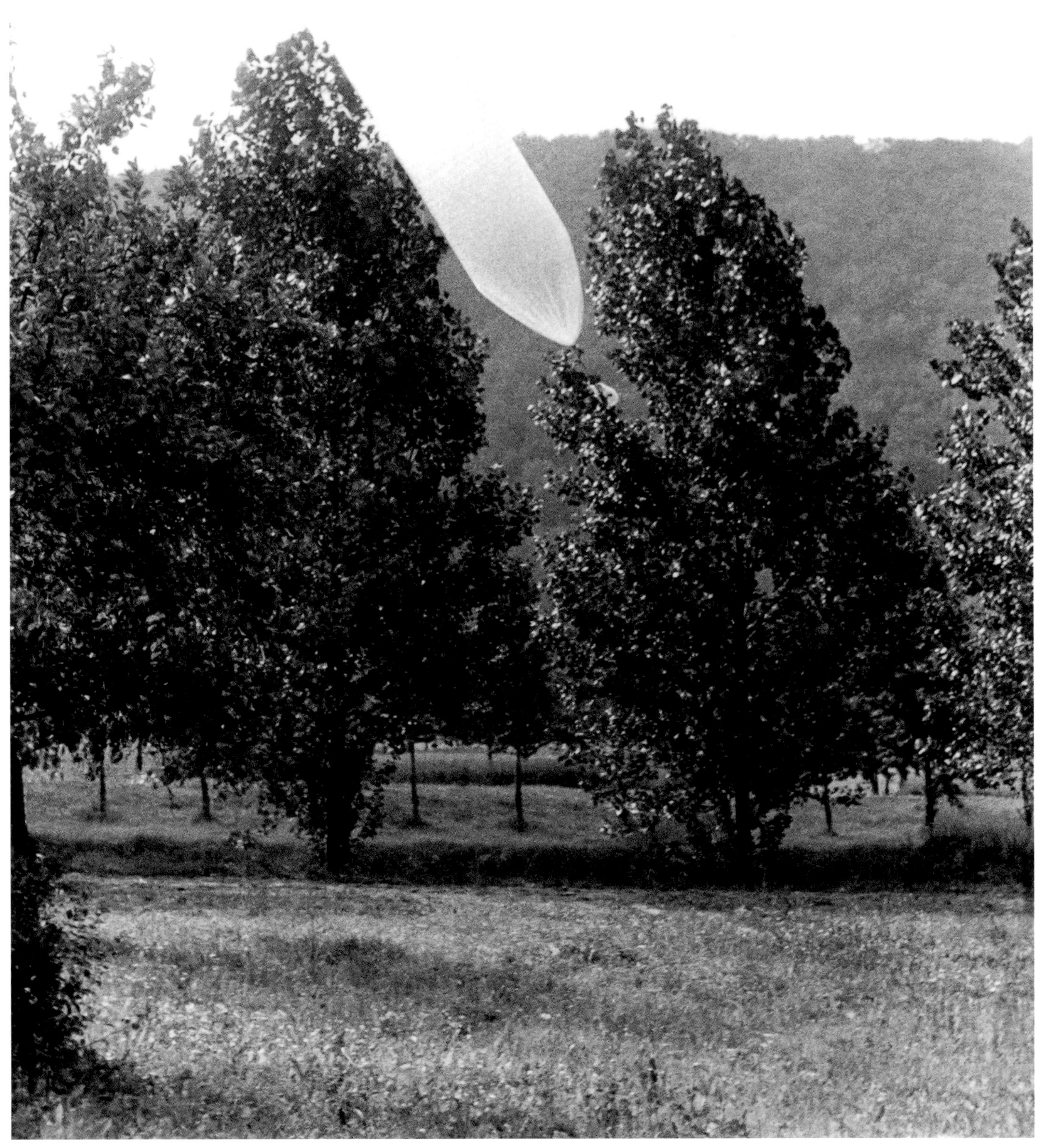

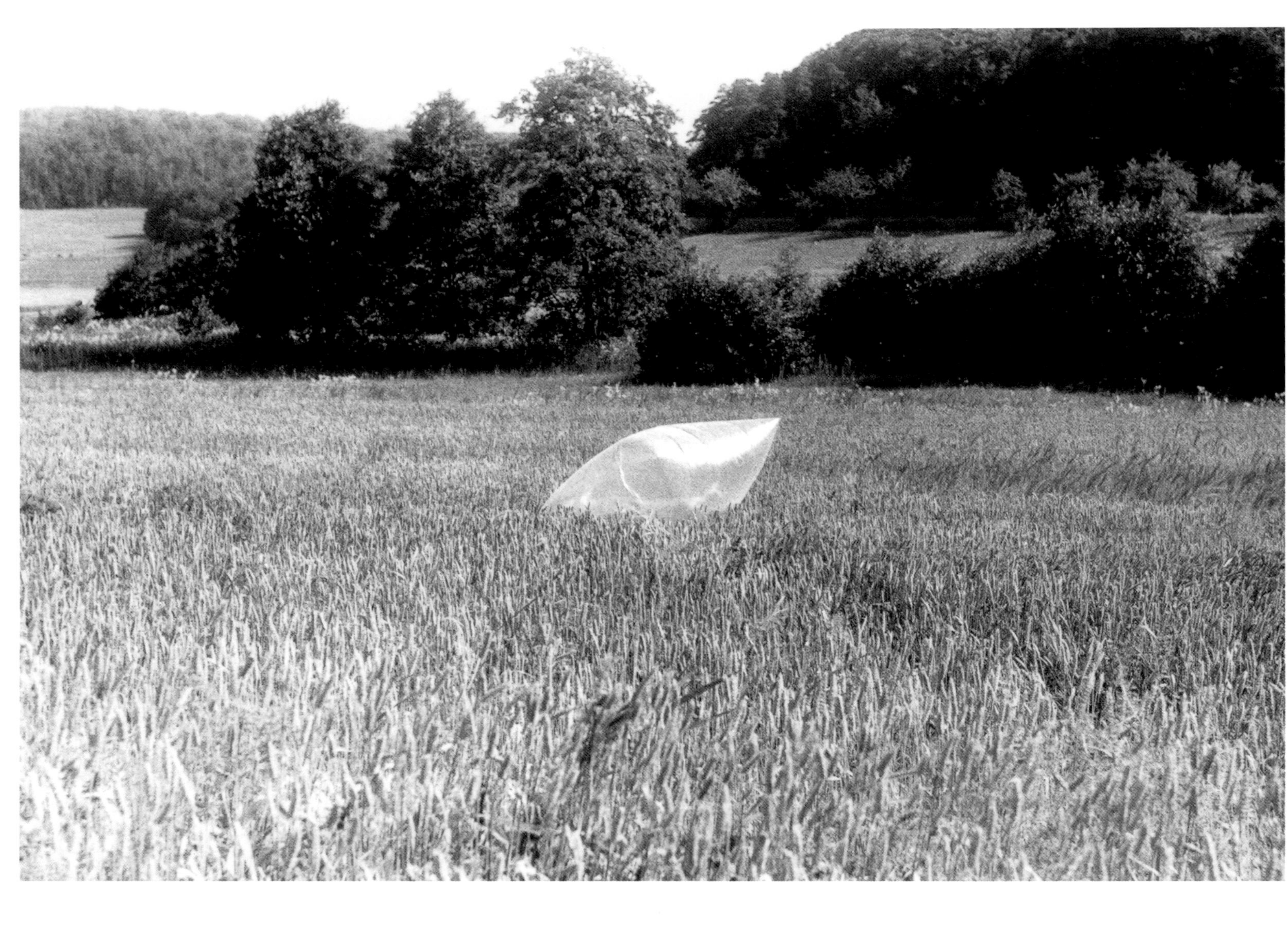

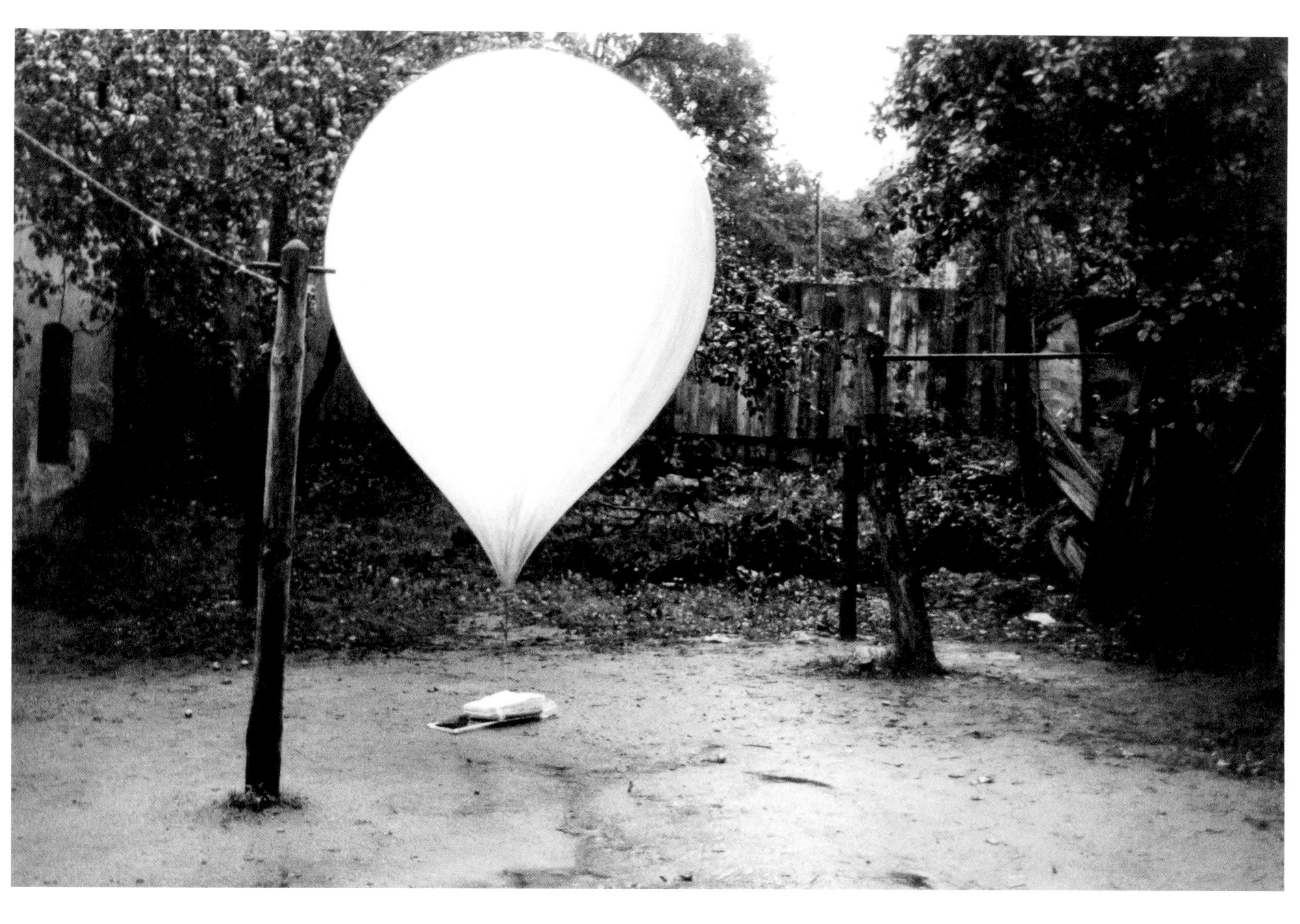

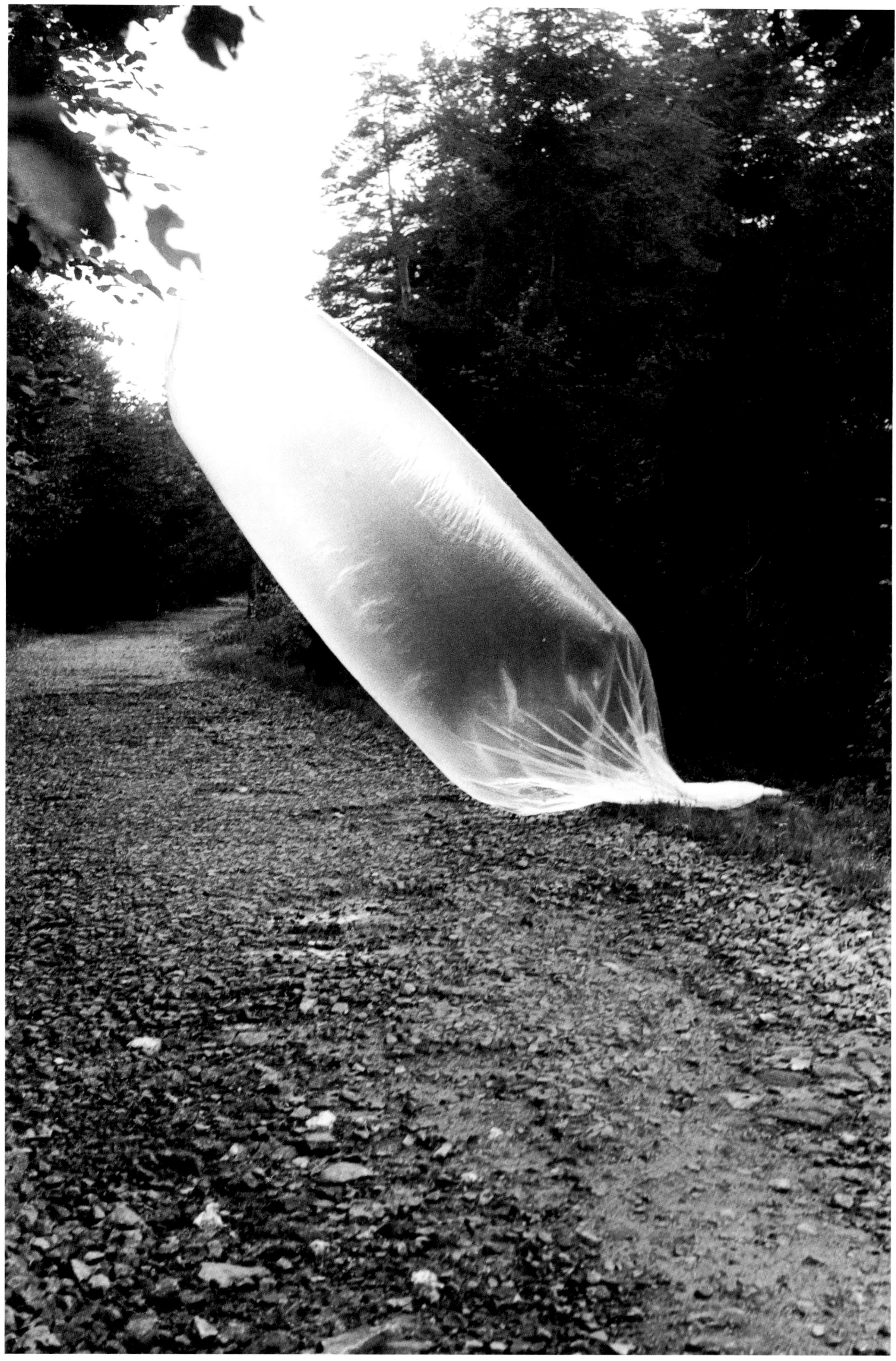

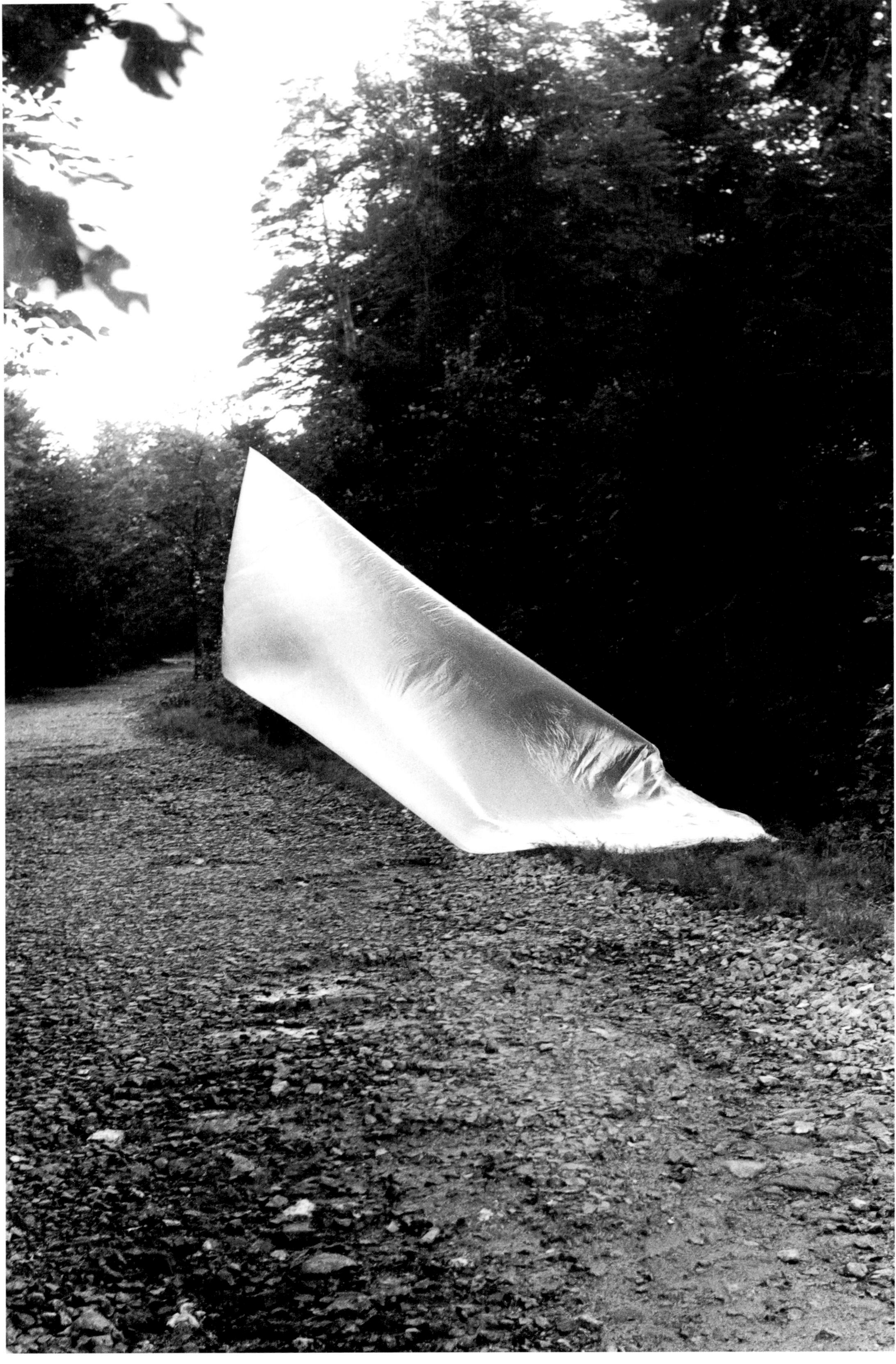

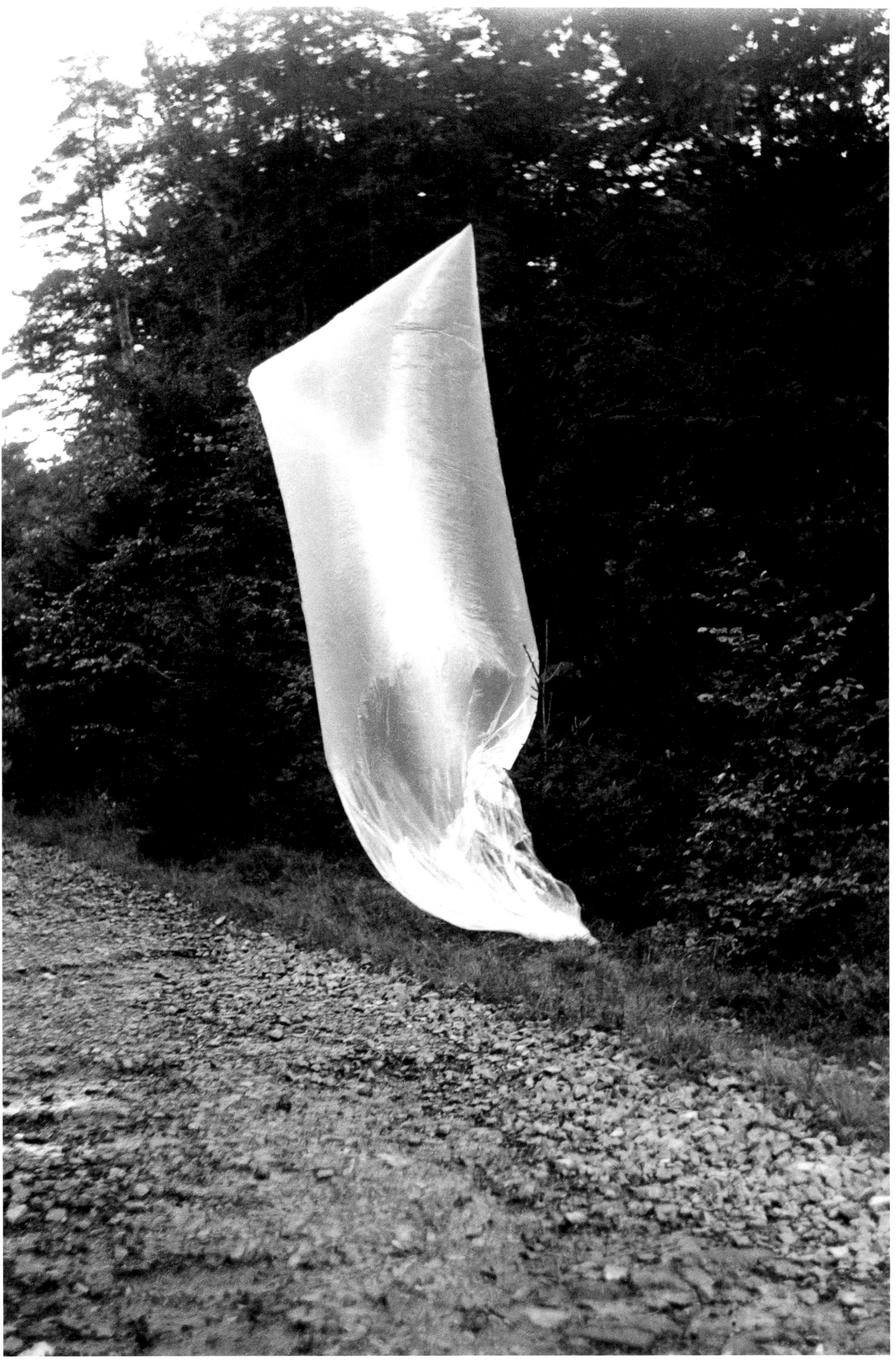

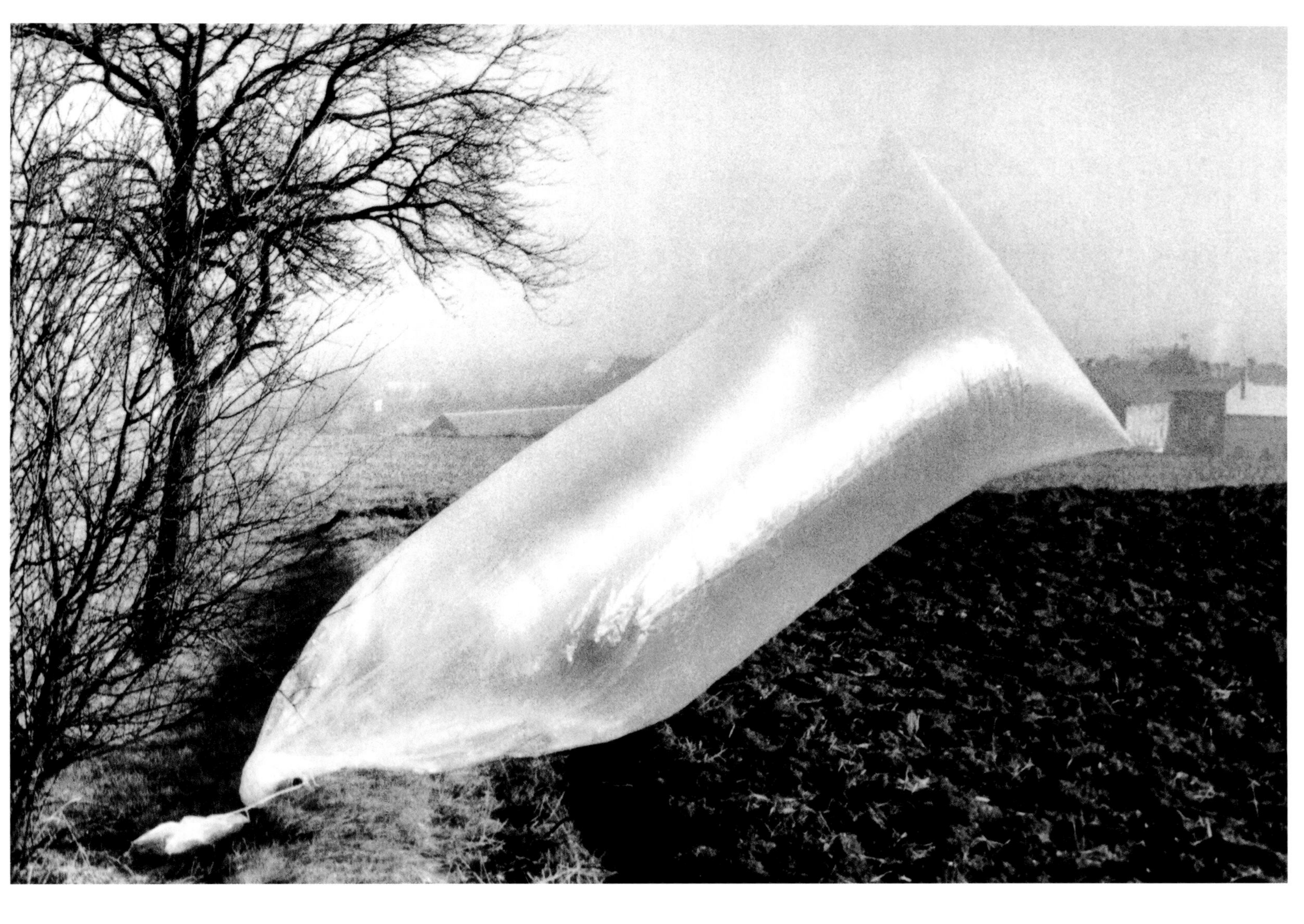

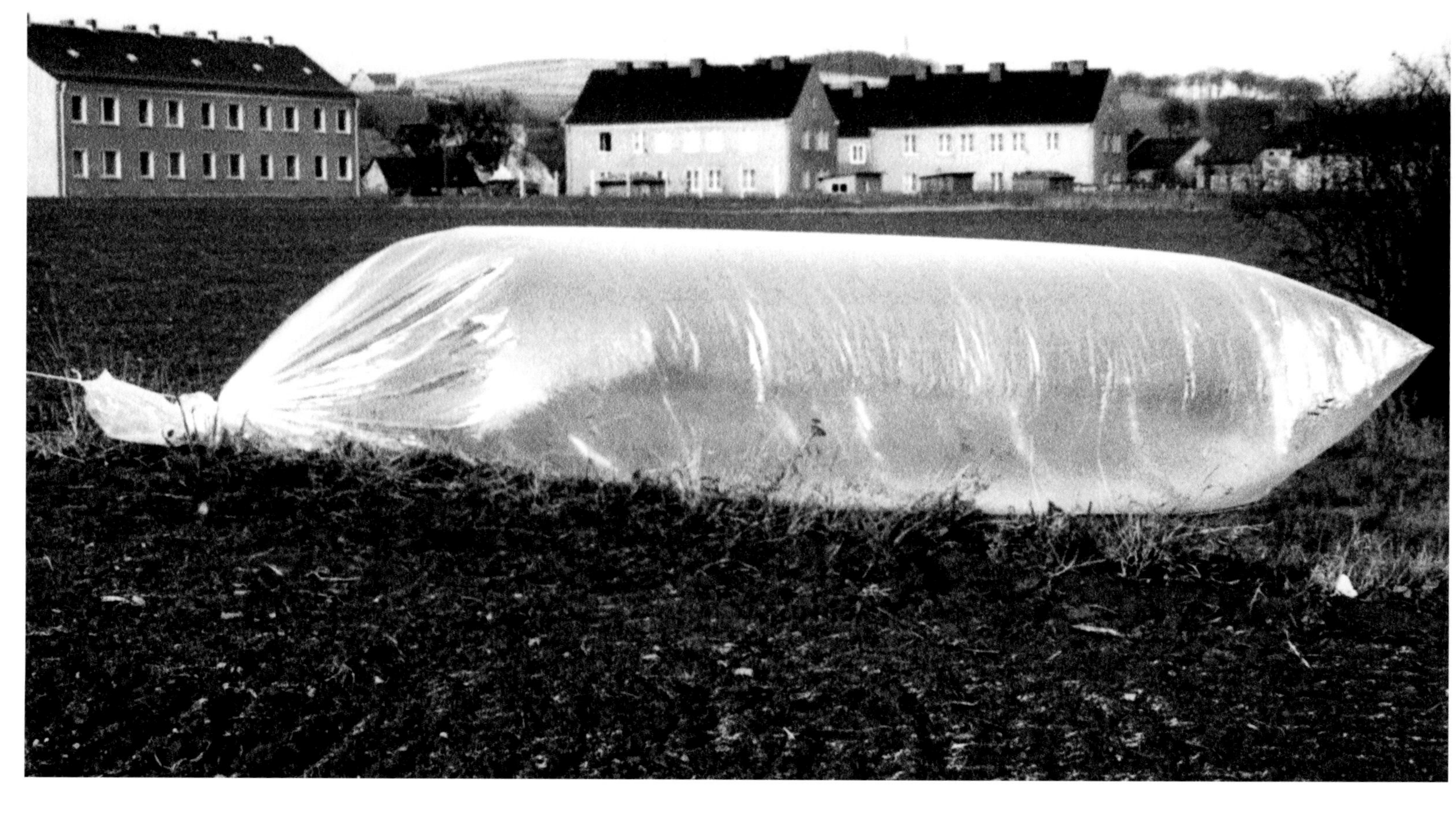

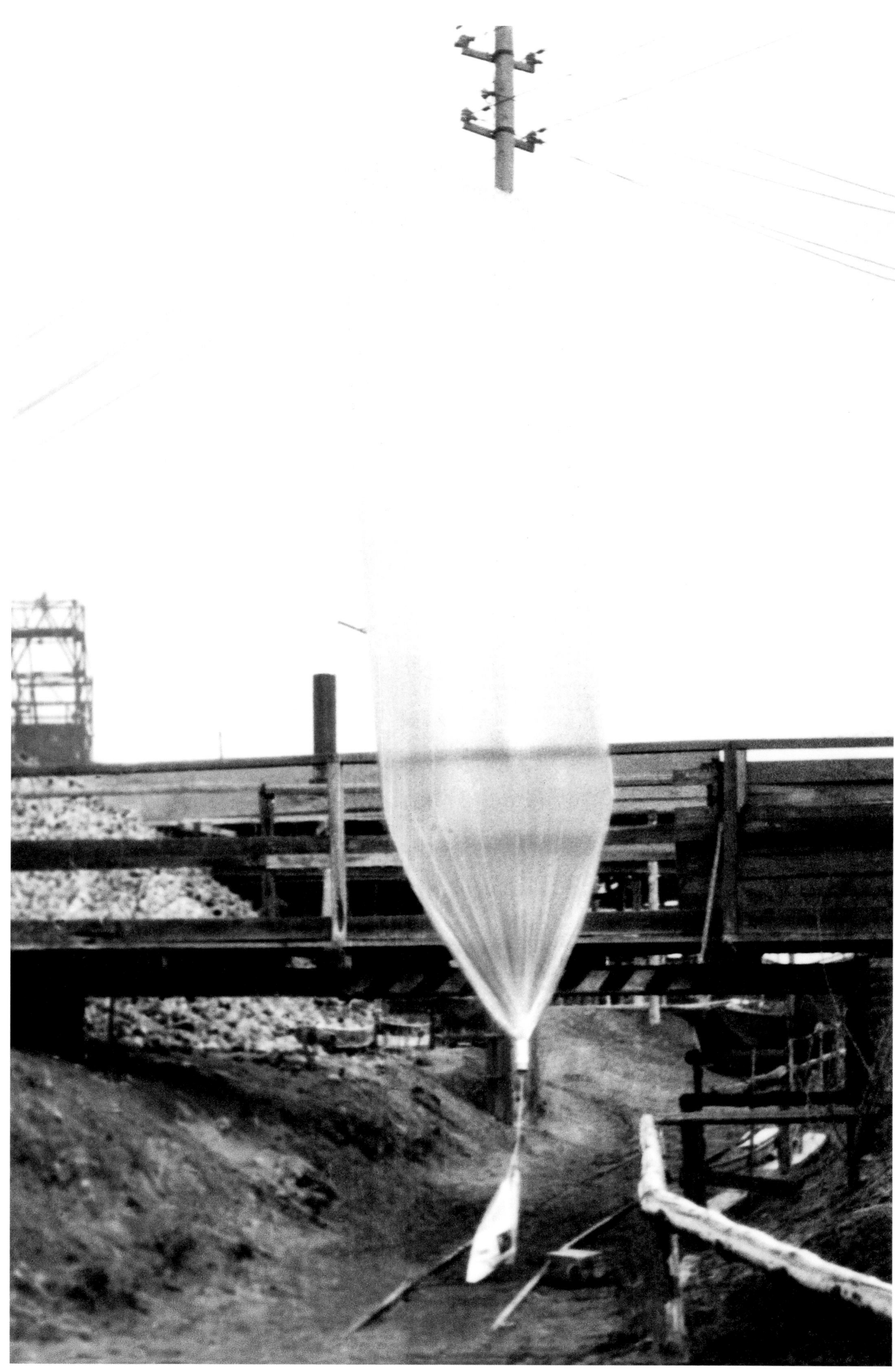

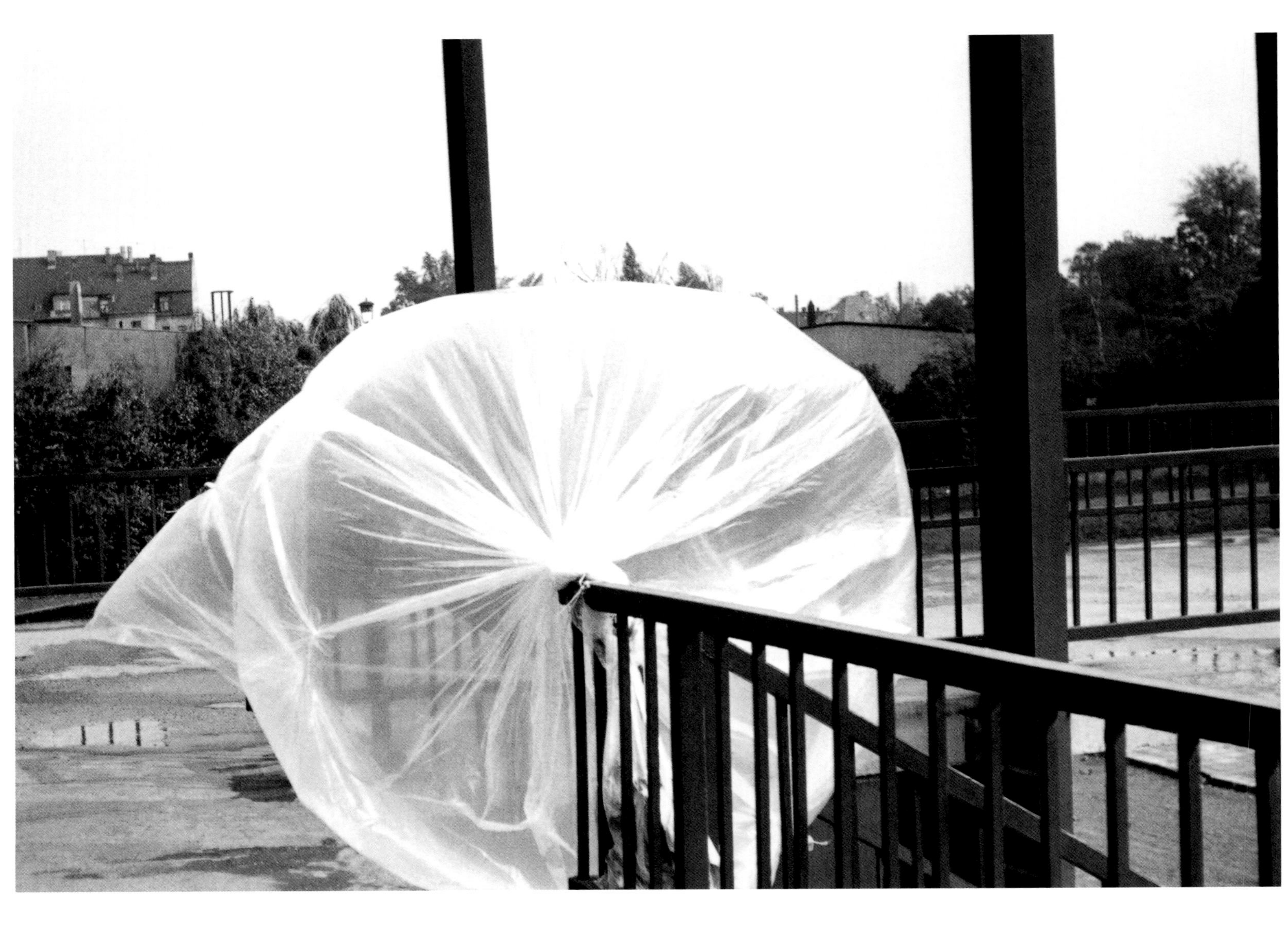

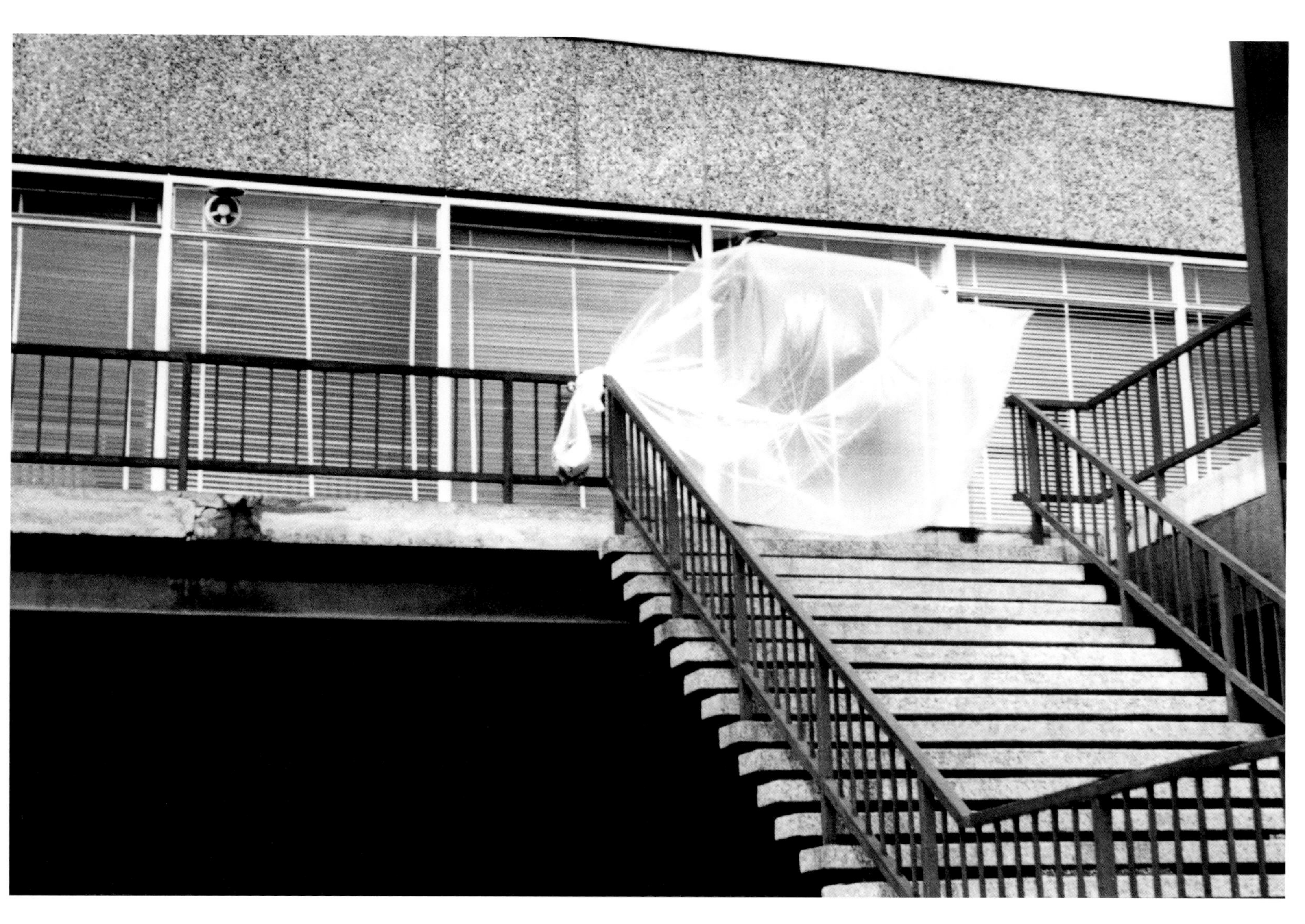

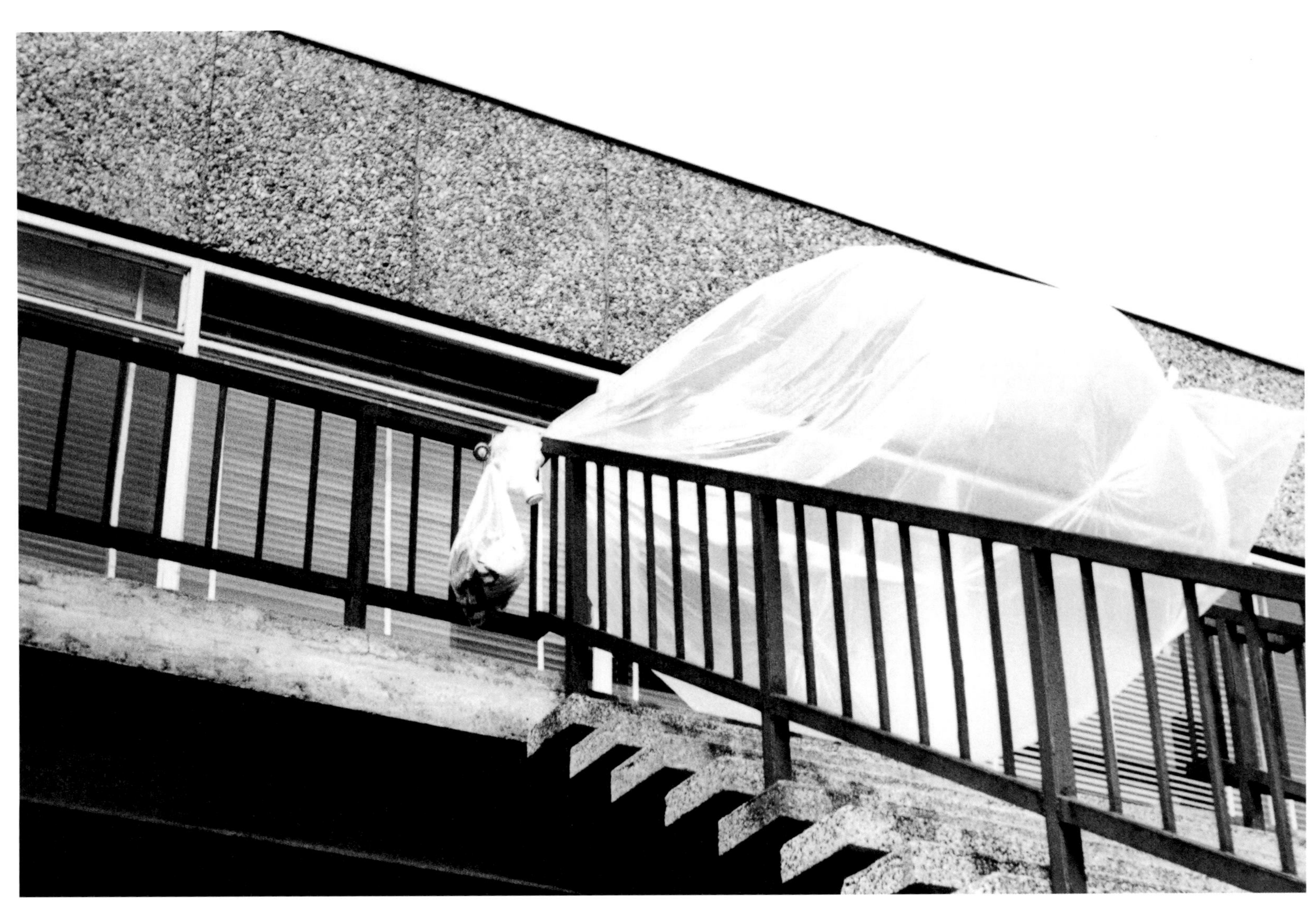

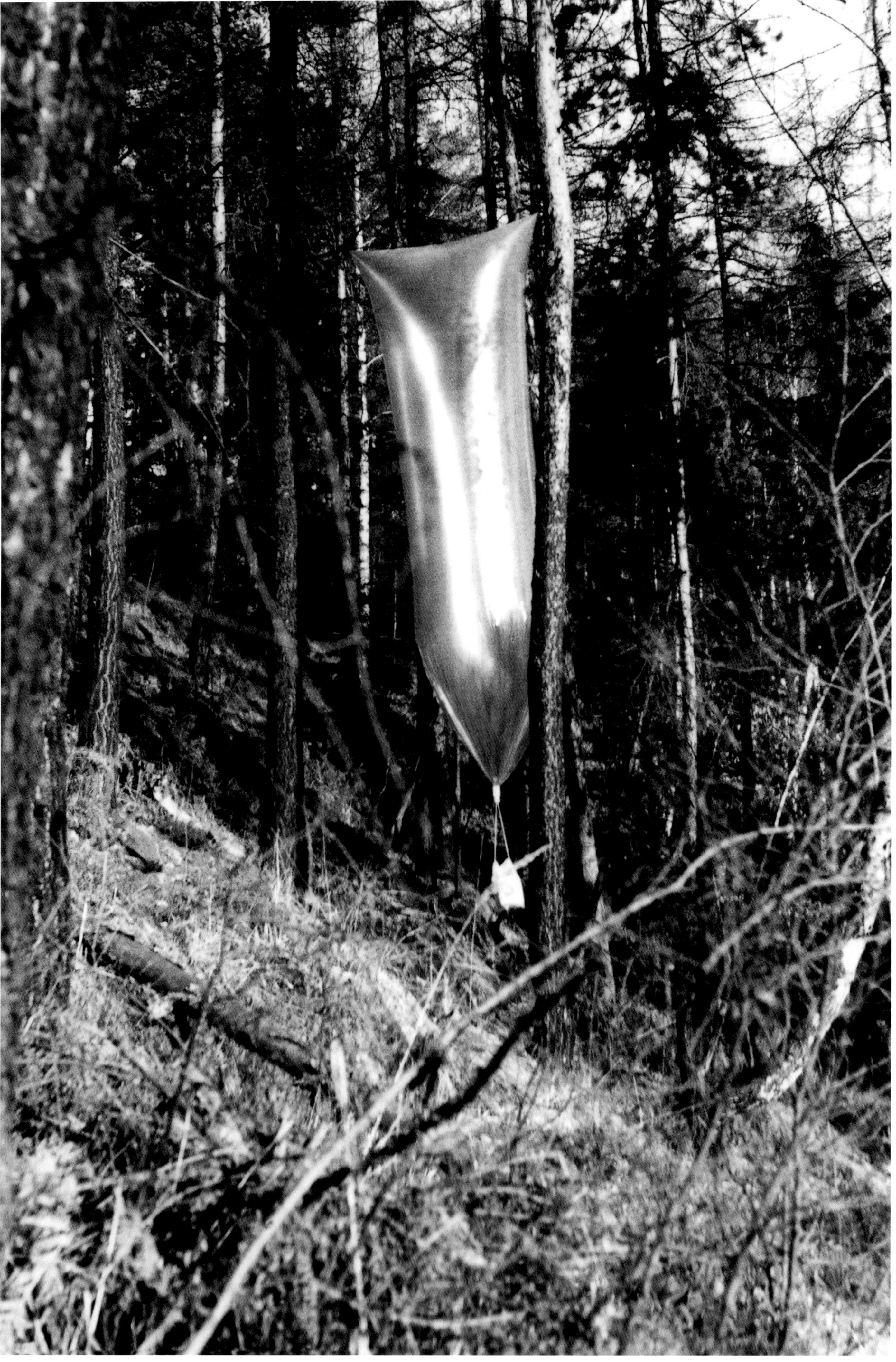

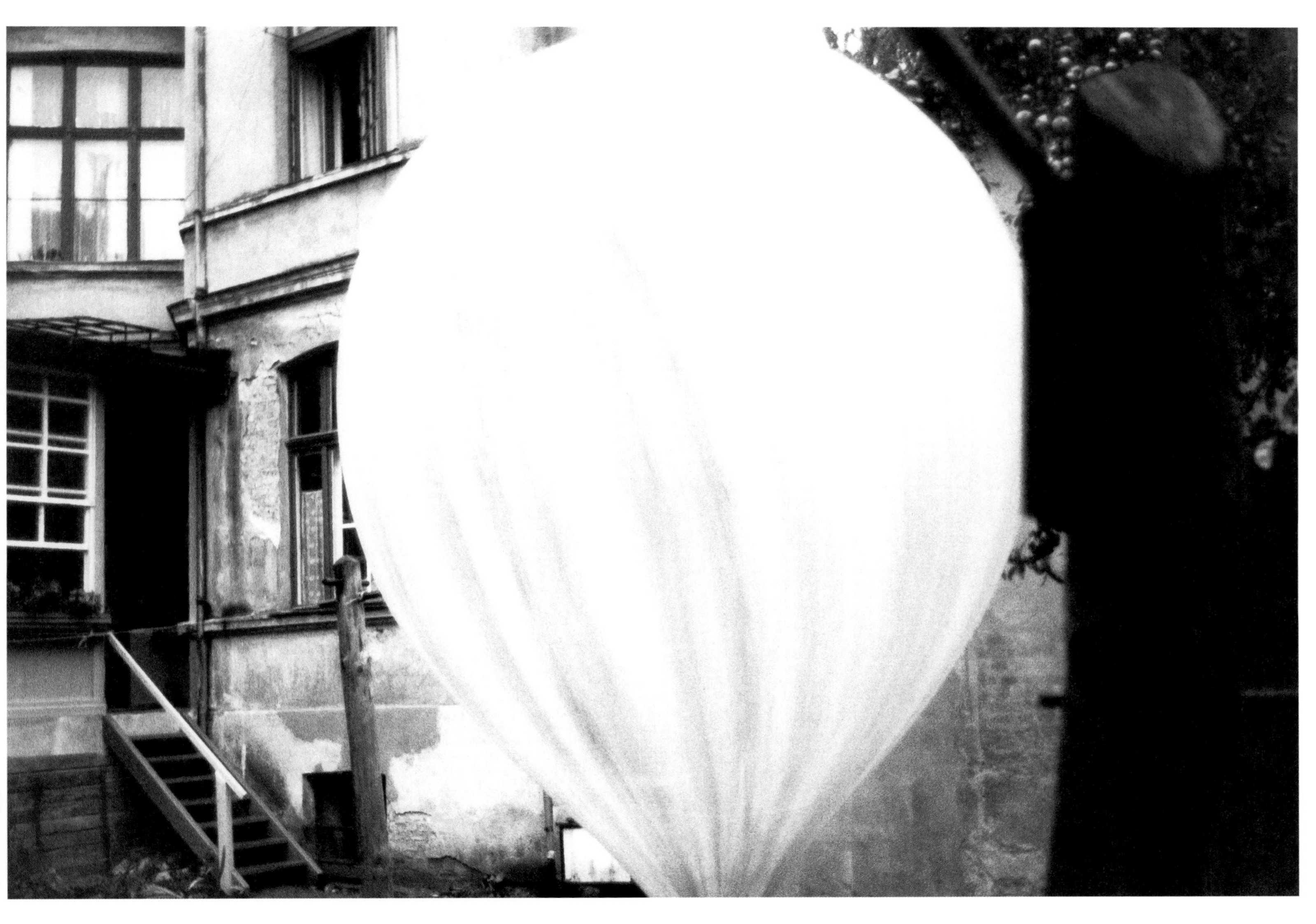

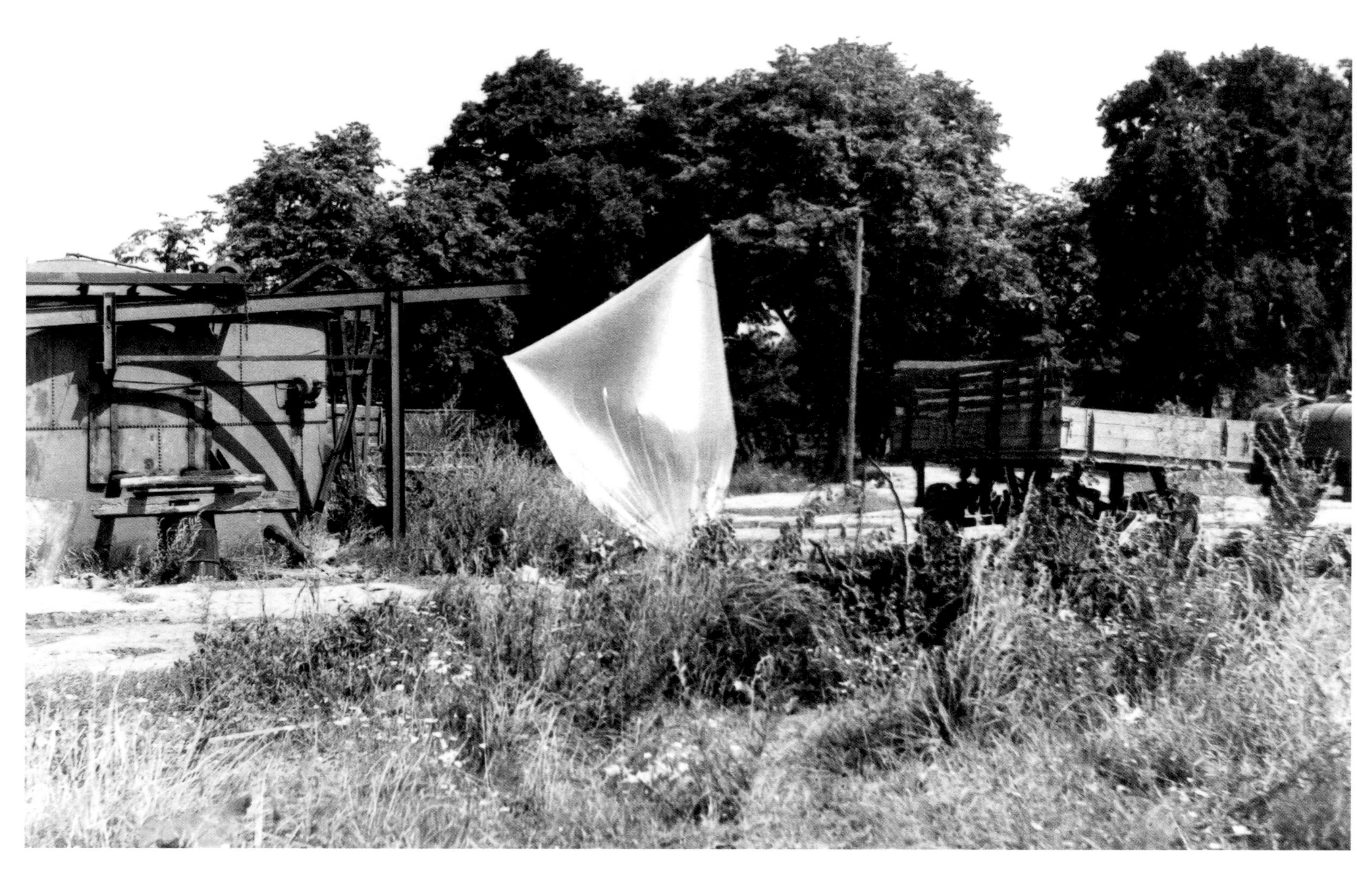

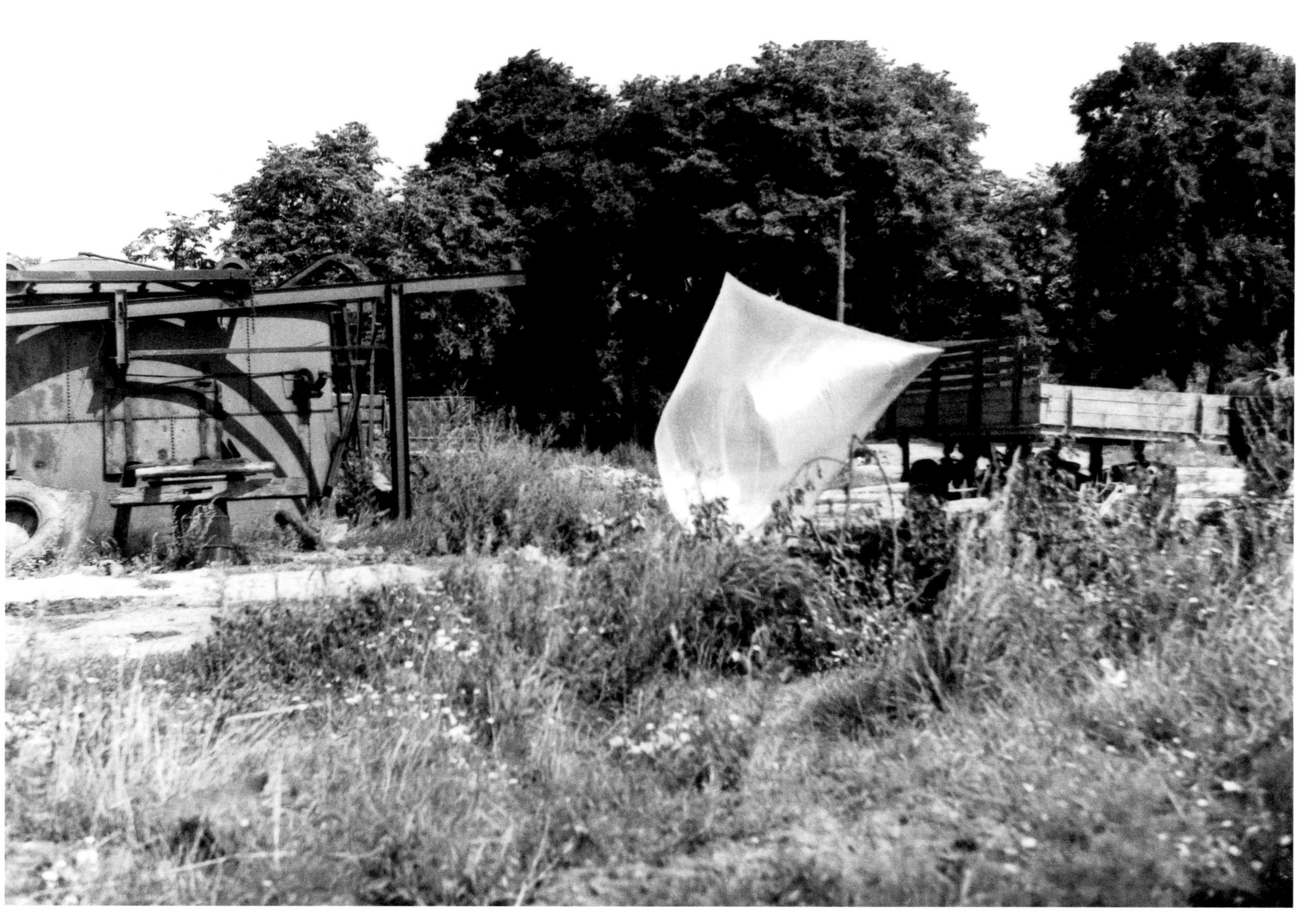

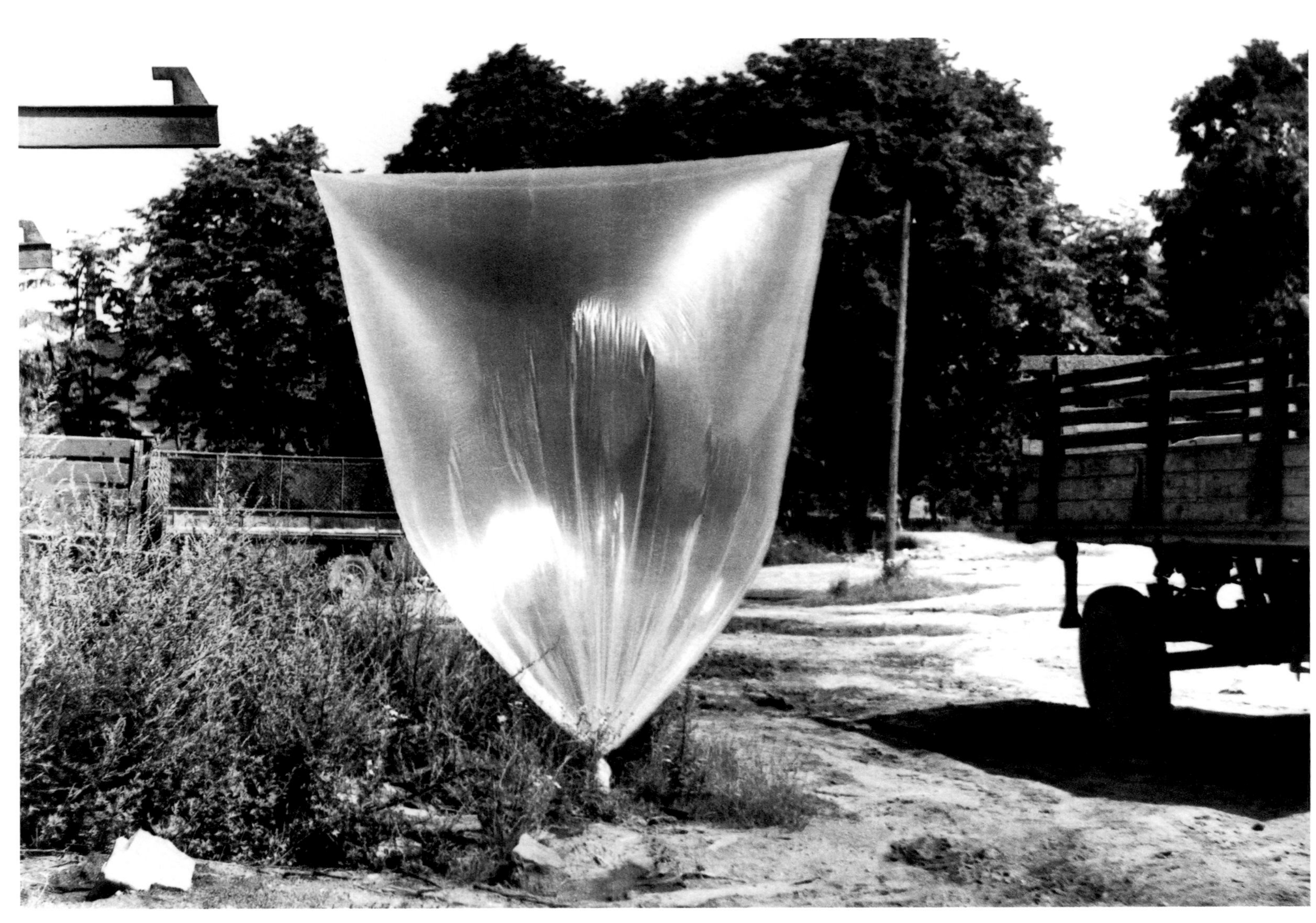

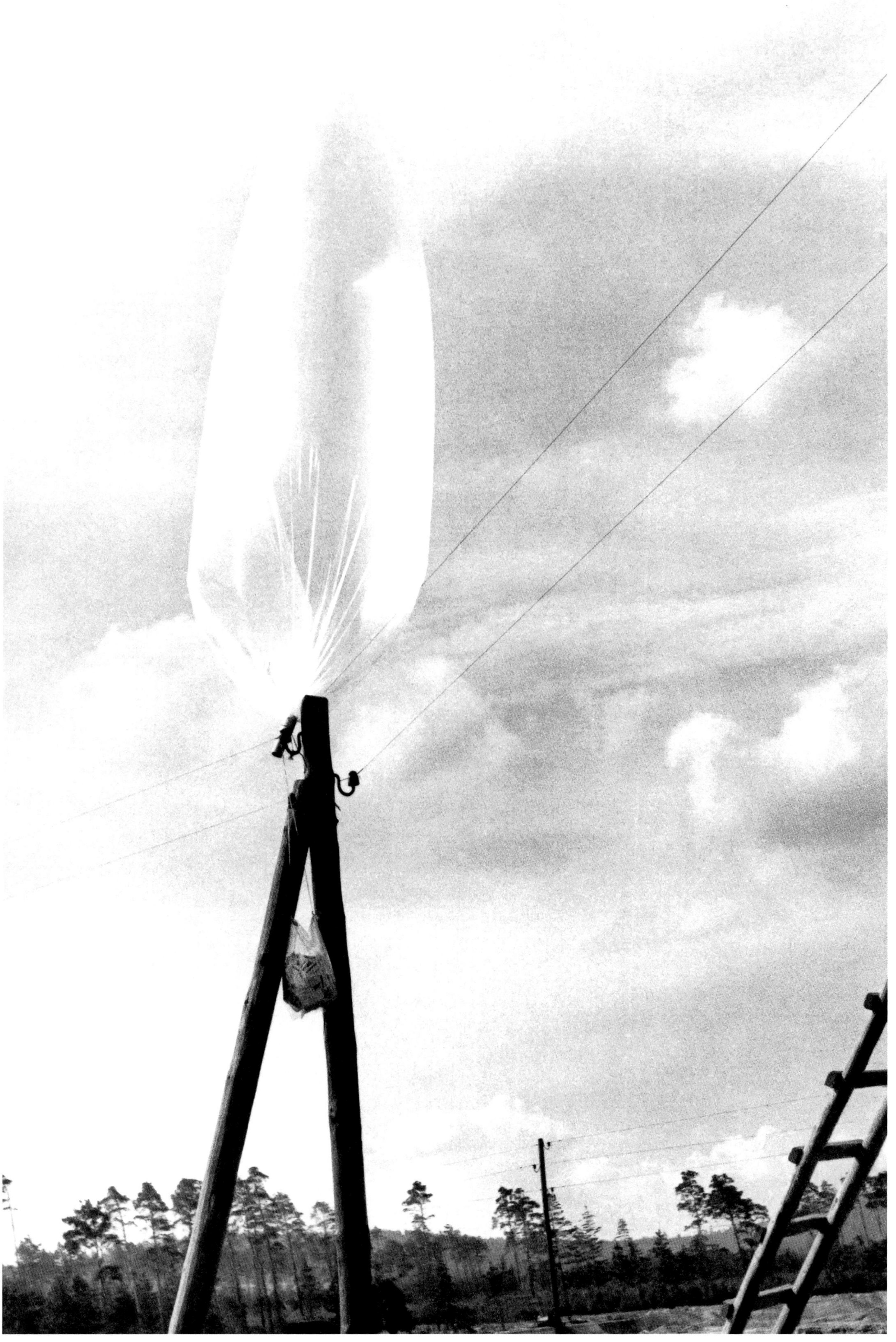

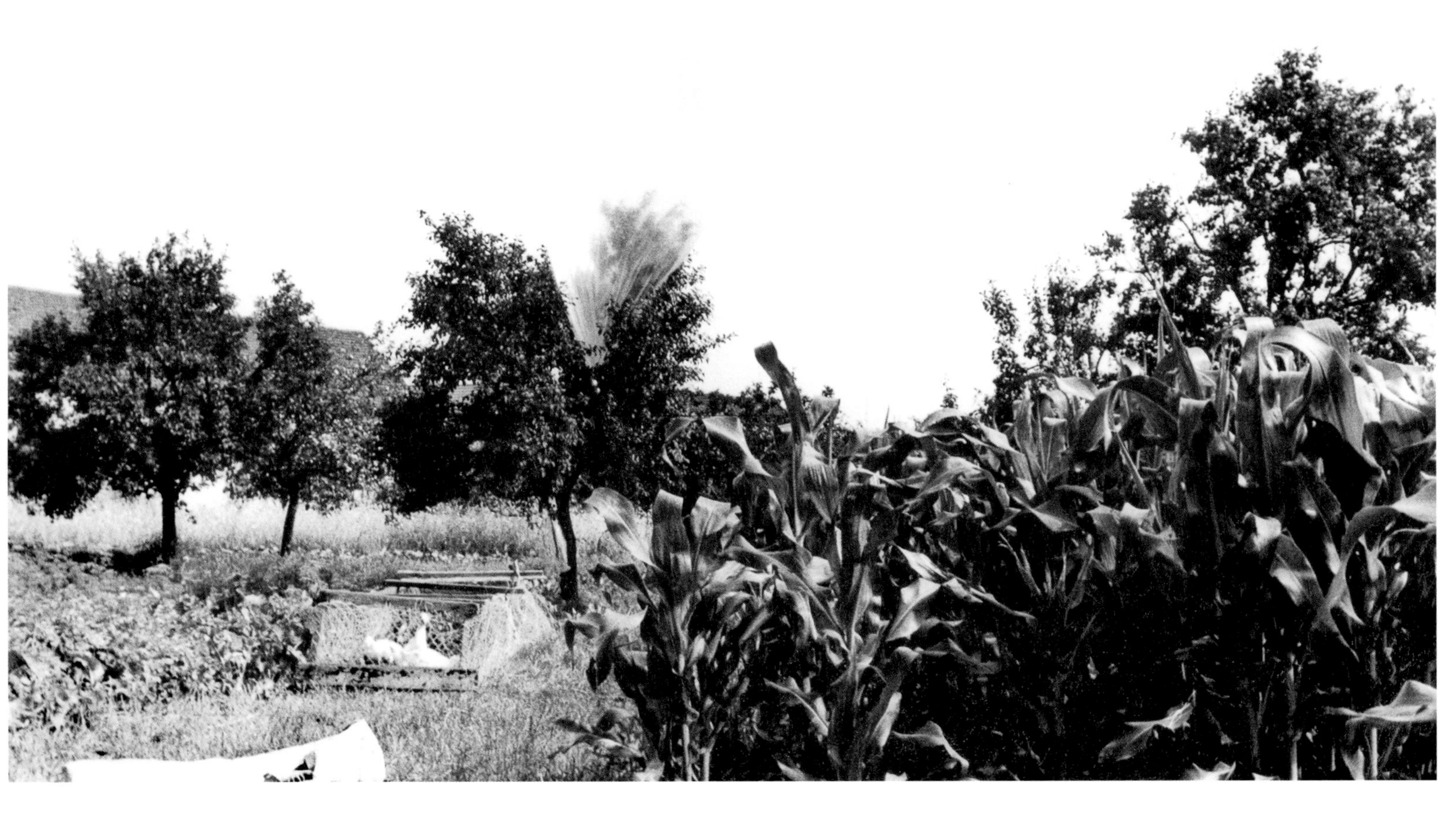

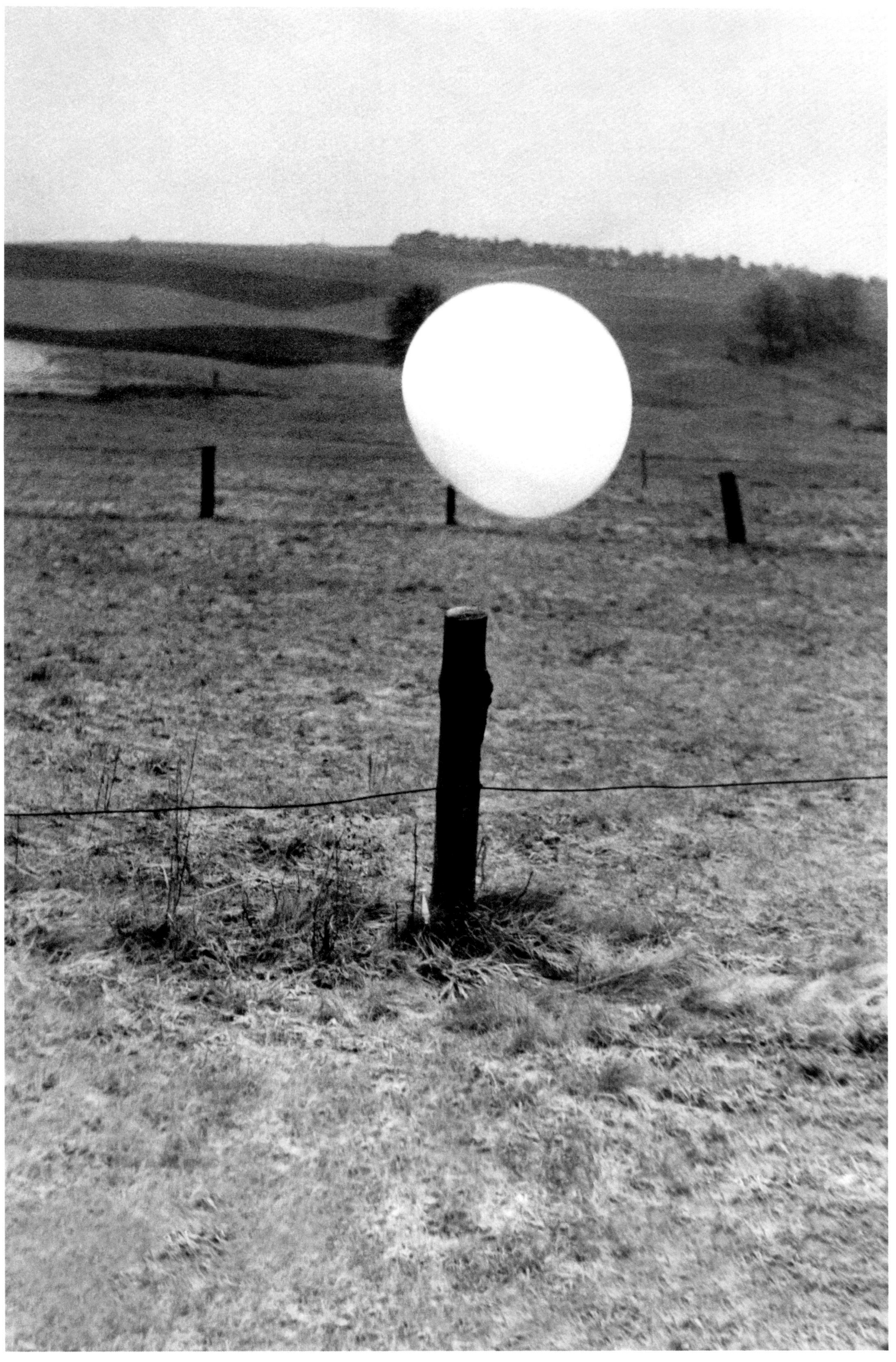

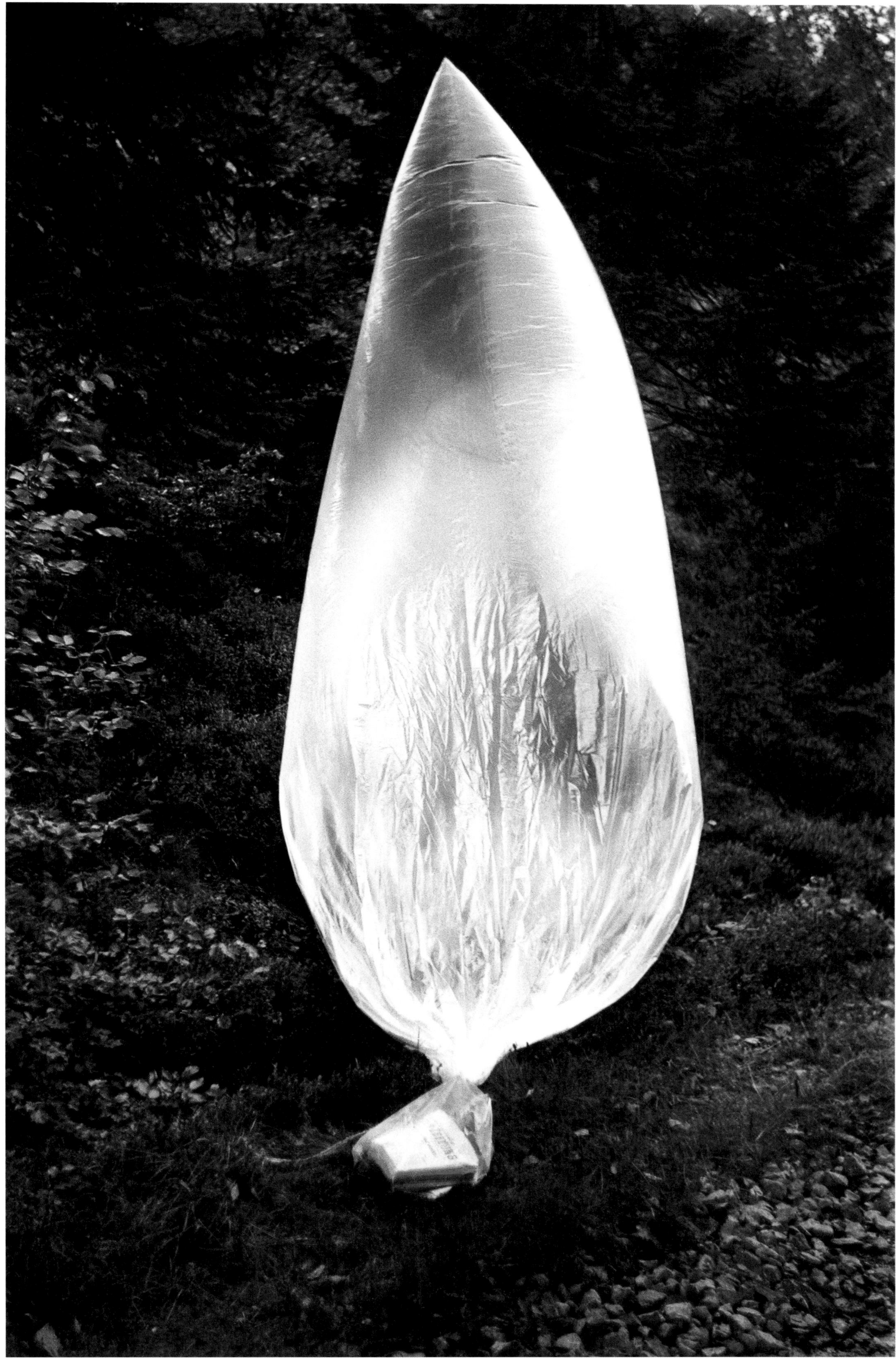

On July 21, 1962 a balloon carrying propaganda pamphlets went down on the main street in Groß Rosenburg Parish, Schönebeck District in close proximity to the Rosenburger Hof Inn. The package it was carrying, containing about a thousand DGB *Freie Tribüne* (Free Tribune) No. 6/61 pamphlets, failed to open. Telephone wires stretching across the street were damaged by the balloon as it went down. Comrade Harry Agthe, LPG chairman, happened to be only three meters away when the balloon hit the sidewalk.

On July 26, 1962 at about 9:00 a.m. a propaganda balloon carrying one hundred pamphlets (*Tribüne*) crashed in the courtyard of a kindergarden in Jänickendorf / Luckenwalde. The package had failed to open. None of the children playing there were injured. The teacher burned all the pamphlets and the balloon carrying them.

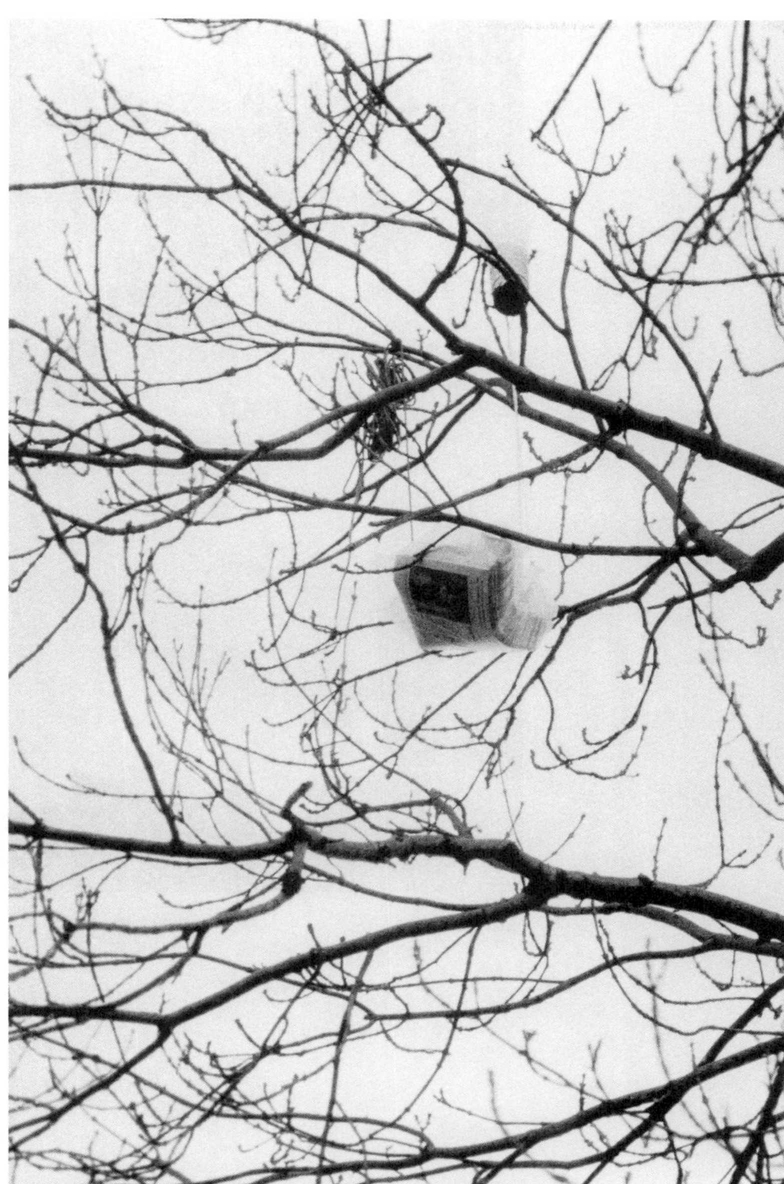

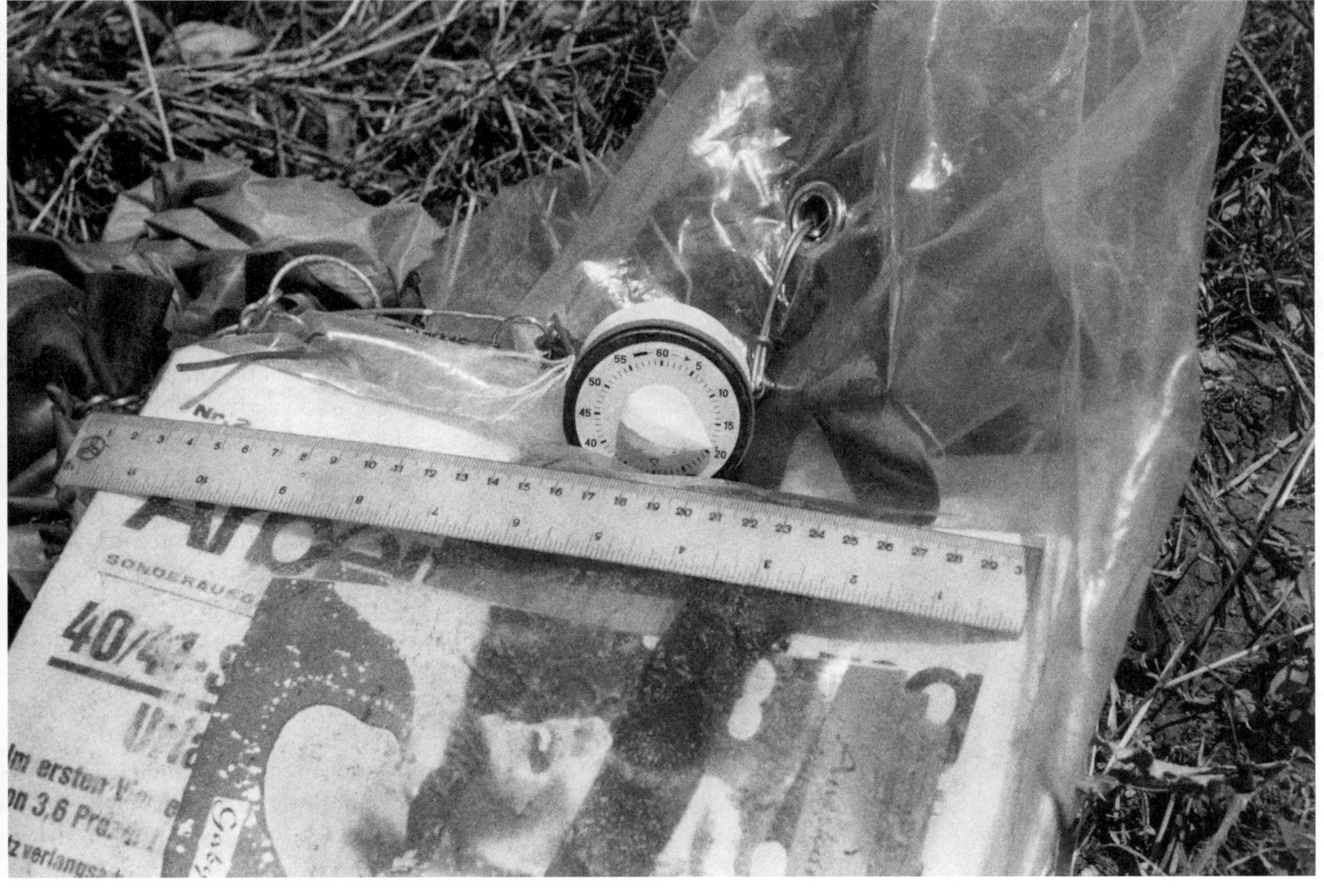

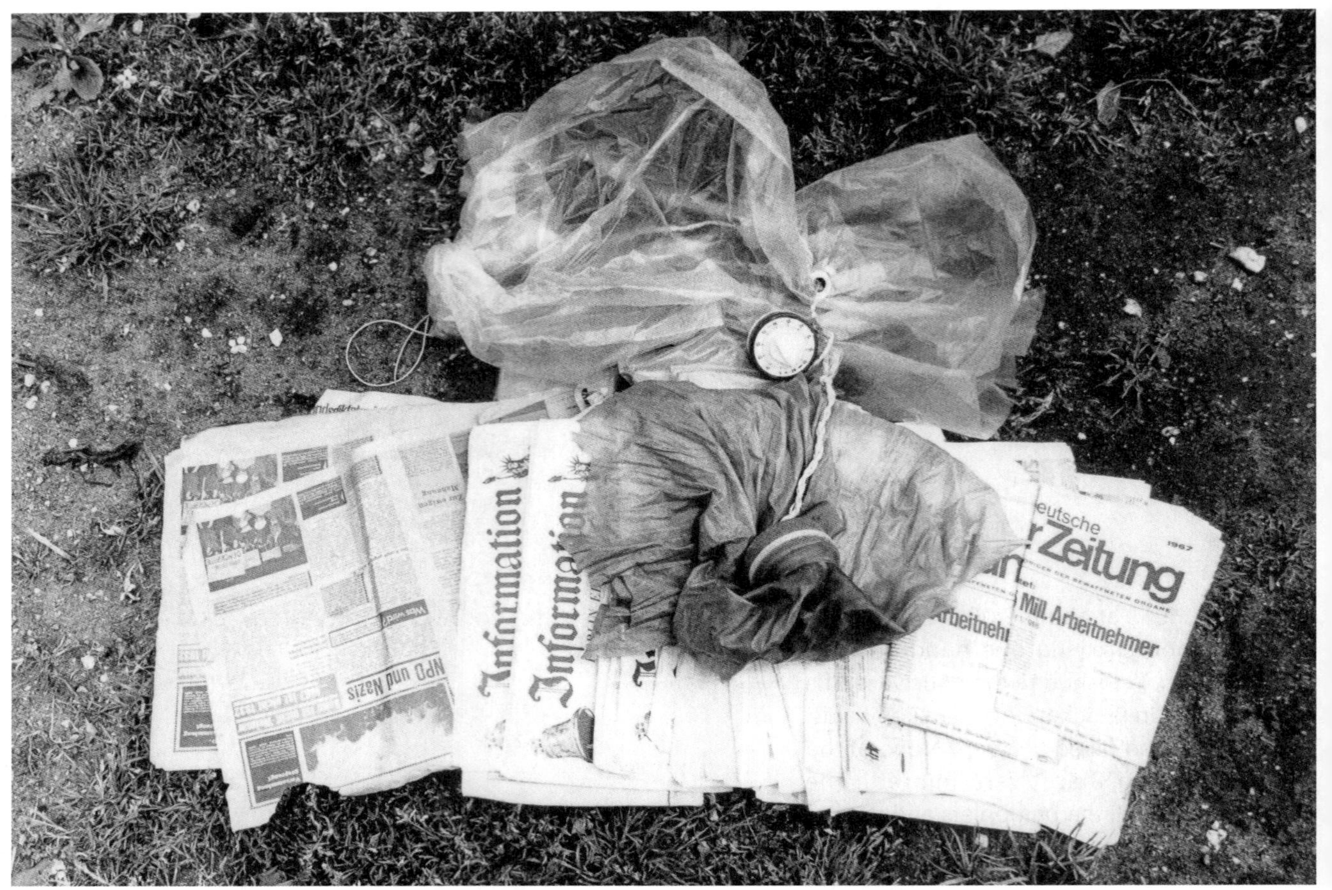

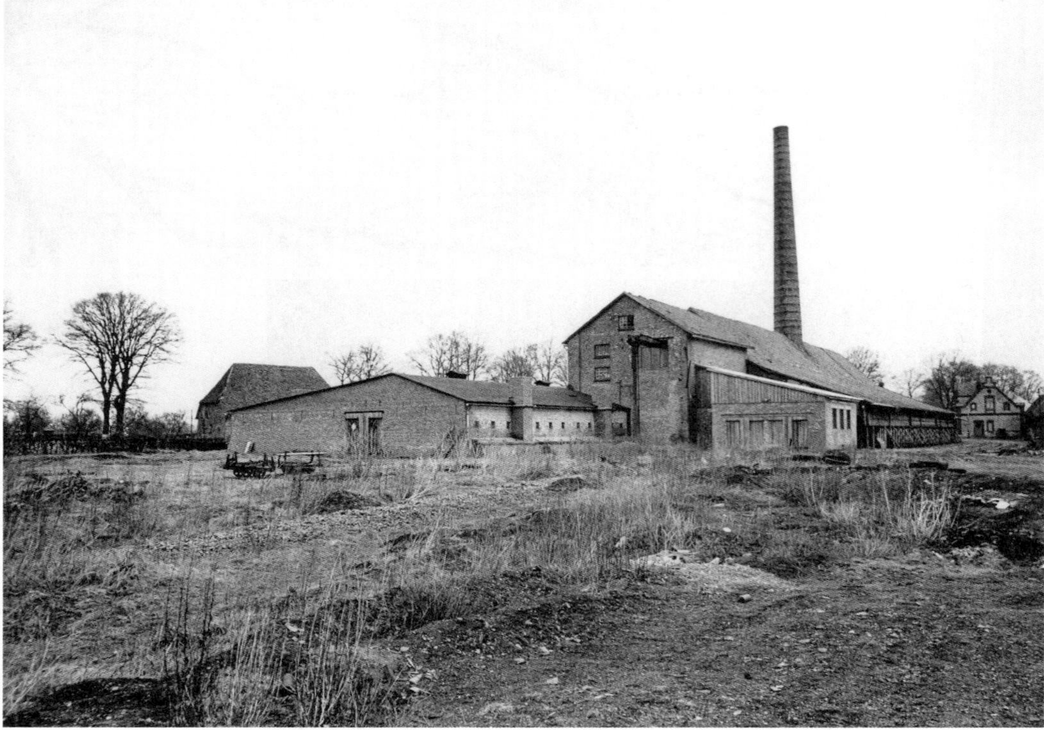

On June 27, 1963, at about 10:00 a.m., the undersigned, Lieutenant Colonel Lutz, was informed on the telephone by the Reconnaissance and Notification Division that a balloon carrying propaganda pamphlets was caught in a tree near the railroad track. A. and M. from the Transport Police received this message. After receipt of the message, a car was sent to the site. The site where it was found was about fifty meters away from the newly built road. The balloon was in the branches of a European oak approximately thirty to thirty-five meters high and roughly 200 to 250 years old. On hitting the ground, the balloon was inflated by the wind and that was how it was found. The oak stands on the right in the property, as viewed from the road. The railroad line runs on the left along the road. The ascent of a comrade with climbing irons was unsuccessful. Since it was impossible to reach the top branches and fire department ladders could not be deployed, a visit was made to the District Forest Ranger. From him the undersigned received the necessary approval to fell the tree. With the help of forestry workers, who had been called in, this was done and the balloon carrying propaganda pamphlets was removed from the crown of the tree. That day the prevailing weather was calm, sunny and with good visibility. The temperature rose during the day from twelve degrees Celsius to twenty-two degrees Celsius. No precipitation was noted. A force three to four westerly wind was blowing.

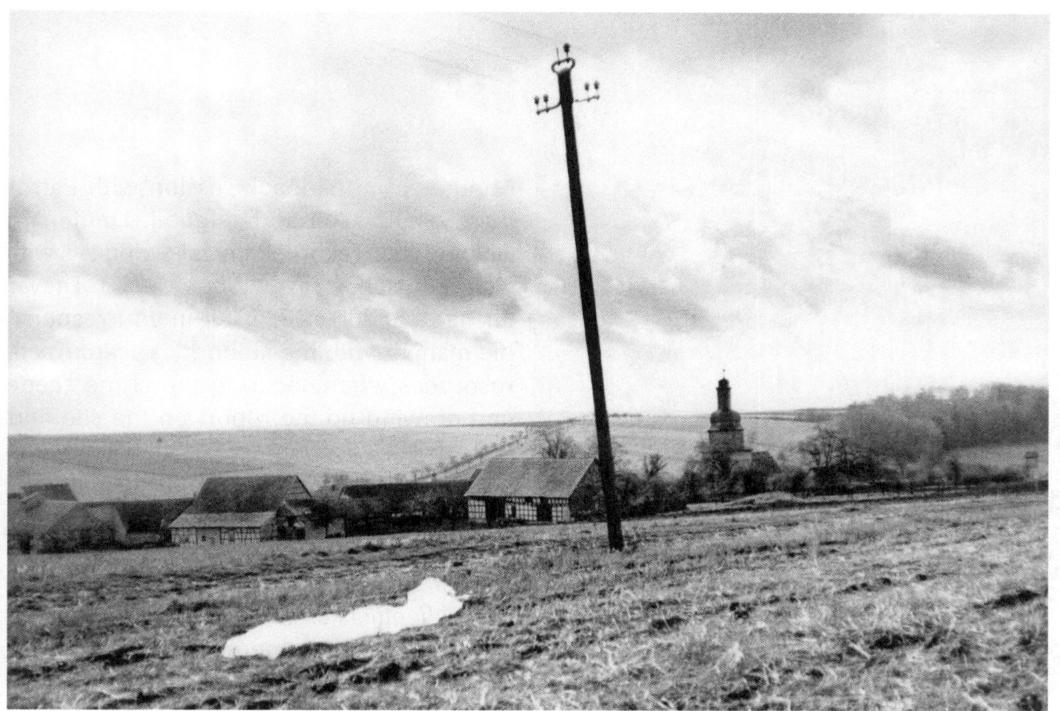

Near the Inselberg, September 20, 1963 in the morning: We should like to inform you that approximately 4,000 to 5,000 propaganda leaflets were found in a package by a class from the Central Vocational School, Weissensee, Thuringia, Sömmerda District, while on a hike to the Inselberg on October 20, 1963. The package revealed no technical additions. Since the next police station was too far away to be informed and since it was a much-frequented public footpath, the director ordered the entire contents to be burned on the spot. The incineration of the material was photographed.

On August 10,1963 around 5:50 a.m. a balloon was noticed hovering approximately five to eight meters above water level over Lake Werbellin, Eberswalde region, Frankfurt (Oder) District. From that altitude a package was detached and fell into the water. The balloon ascended again and departed the scene heading for Joachimsthal.

On August 13, 1963 Hermann Fischer from Heinzendorf, Wolmirstedt region, was hoeing in his garden between 6:30 and 6:45 a.m. During that time a package with propaganda pamphlets fell to the ground near him.

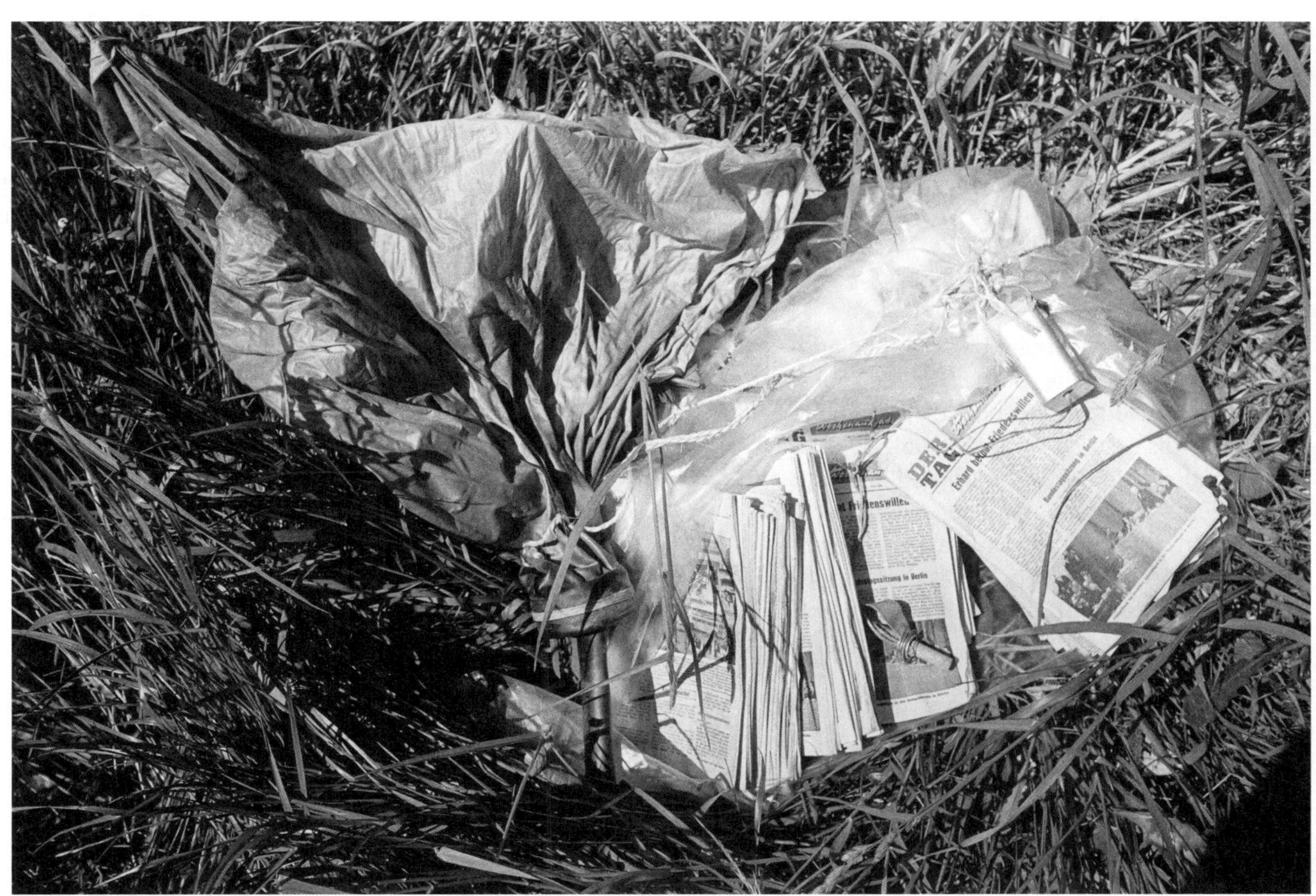

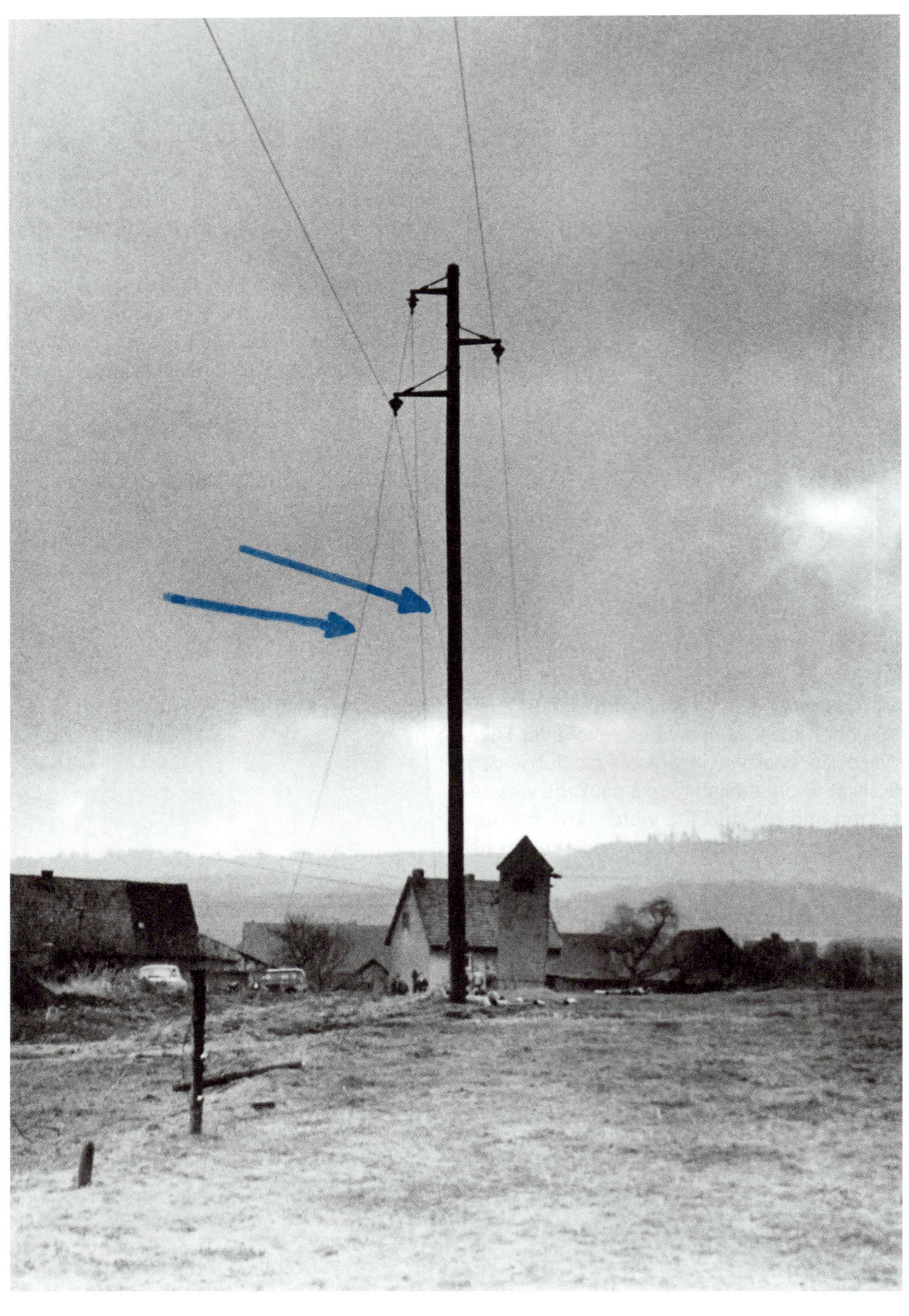

In the time between November 28, 1964 and December 1, 1964 quite a large leafleting campaign was started on the part of the adversary in Worbis District. Approximately 30,000 propaganda leaflets were smuggled in using a large number of balloons. The leaflets were strewn across the land of twenty-one communities. The community of Bischofferode and the Thomas Müntzer potash works were most severely affected. School classes were deployed for several days to search for the leaflets that had come down.

Minutes of a feedback session with Patrolman Schulz: The undersigned, Lieutenant Colonel Lutz, recorded the following talk with Comrade Schulz on October 6, 1963. The latter had conducted himself in an irresponsible manner with the authority's scarce state resources when securing the crime scene and drawing up the report on the site findings. The text was prepared after a balloon carrying approximately 4,000 propaganda leaflets and weighing approximately five kilograms came down near Zella-Mehlis on September 9, 1963. Contents: *Legal Handeln vor aller Öffentlichkeit* (Legal Public Action), instead of the usual one or two photographs, he took innumerable pictures of one and the same balloon. He justified the measure with the excuse that it had been impossible for him to reproduce all aspects of the balloon with a single photograph. This was because the balloon constantly moved and changed shape due to a steady west wind. Analysis of the result produced ten exposed rolls of 35 mm film with 36 exposures each. Since ninety-five balloons carrying propaganda leaflets had gone down in the same timespan within a radius of twenty-five kilometers, those sites could not be photographed because the entire stock of negative film had been used up. Allowances are being made for Comrade Schulz because he is a young colleague and it was his first assignment in the field of forensic science. What was regarded worrying, however, is that colleagues at the site reported that he did not respond to them while the photographs were being taken and was constantly in motion around the balloon carrying propaganda leaflets. In a meeting afterwards Comrade Schulz persisted in his opinion and revealed himself to be unrelenting when confronted with his misconduct. His incomprehension was such that he stated that he would conduct himself in the same way on his next assignment. His class loyalty and his work in the division to date have been impeccable. That the following day was Republic Day was not ignored in the analysis. After a thorough feedback session, it was decided not to issue a written warning letter yet further activity on his part in the forensic science division has been suspended for the time being.

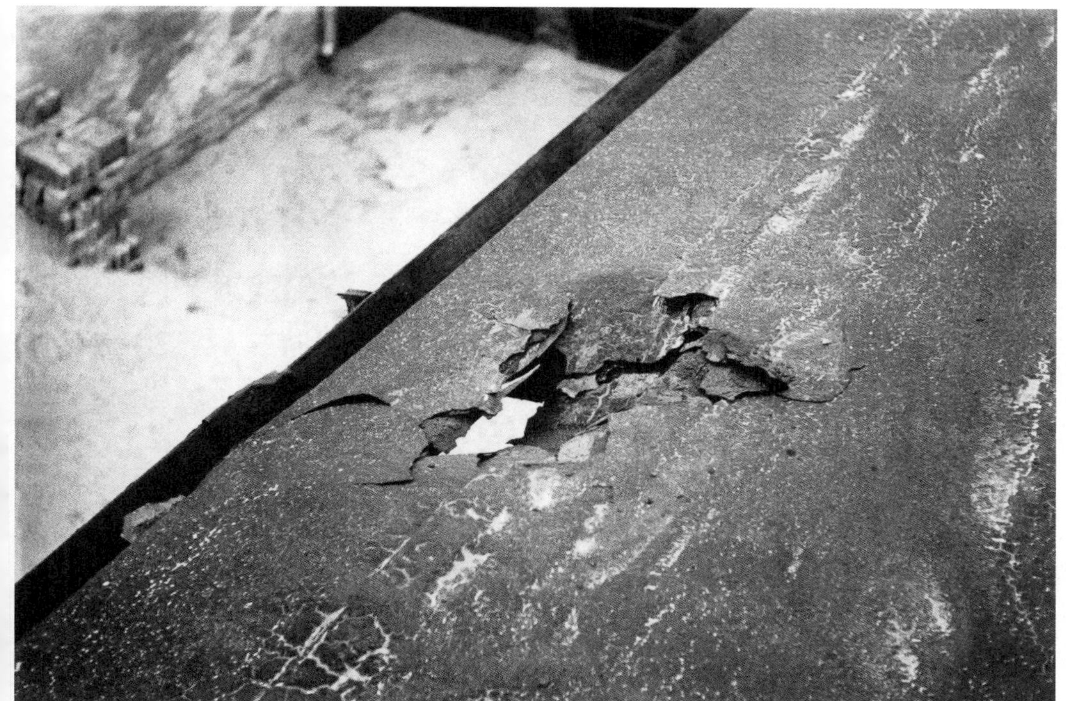

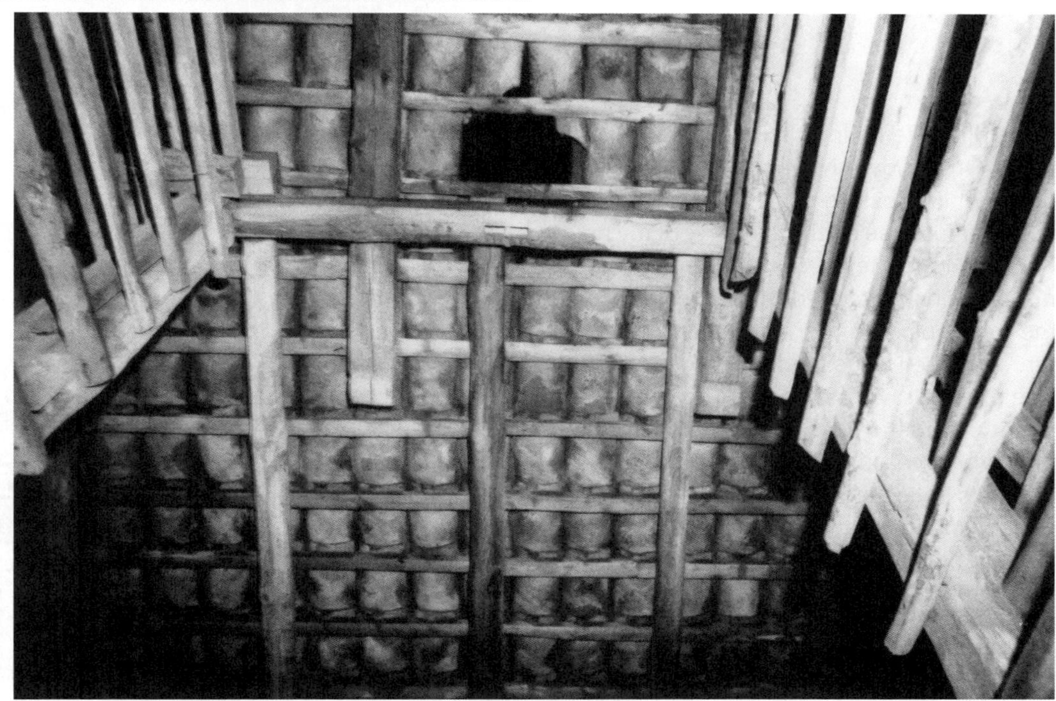

On May 30, 1965 Heinz Konnerth, a collective farmer from Trebula, found a balloon carrying approximately 700 propaganda leaflets in his fruit orchard. Photographs were taken of the site and a statement taken from Konnerth. He is a Party member and a former resettler from Poland. Further, he is known to watch West television and has behaved negatively at Party meetings. Due to his vacillating stance, a personal opinion has been withheld. Konnerth feels that actions of this kind endanger aviation security, only exacerbates tensions between the two German states, and, had the balloon gone down fifty meters from where it did, would have damaged his greenhouse. Since his reputation in the community is not good, publication in the press is inadvisable. Attached we are sending you the negative and three prints as well as the balloon and the propaganda leaflets.

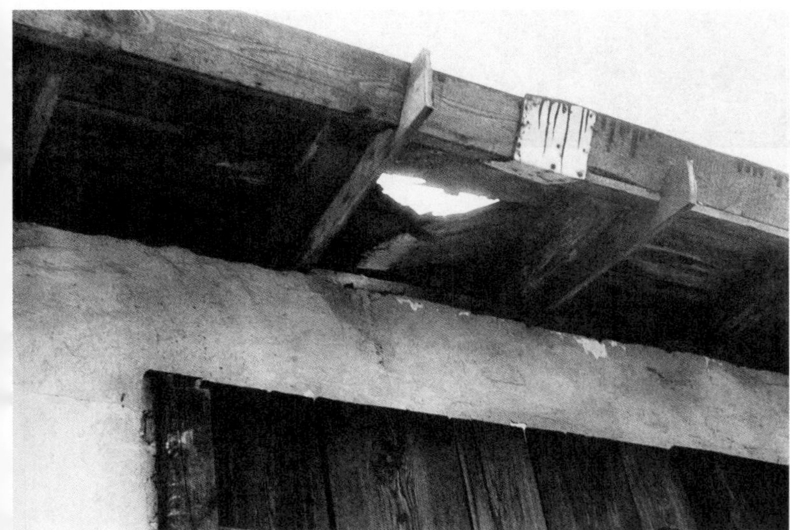

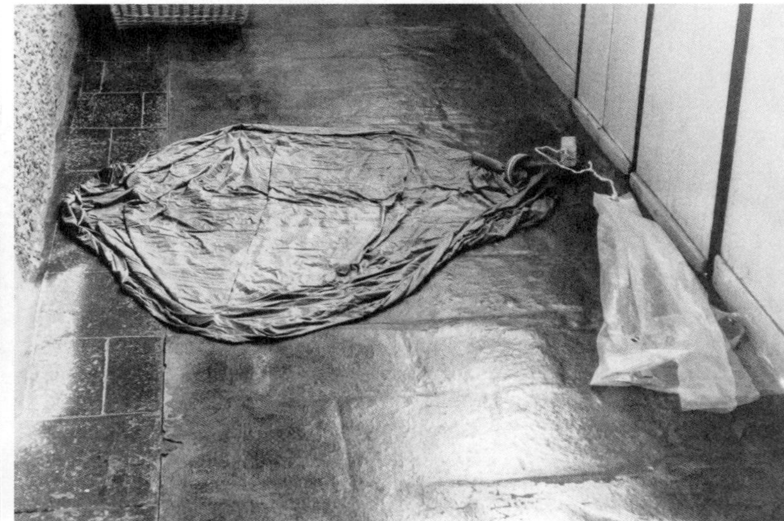

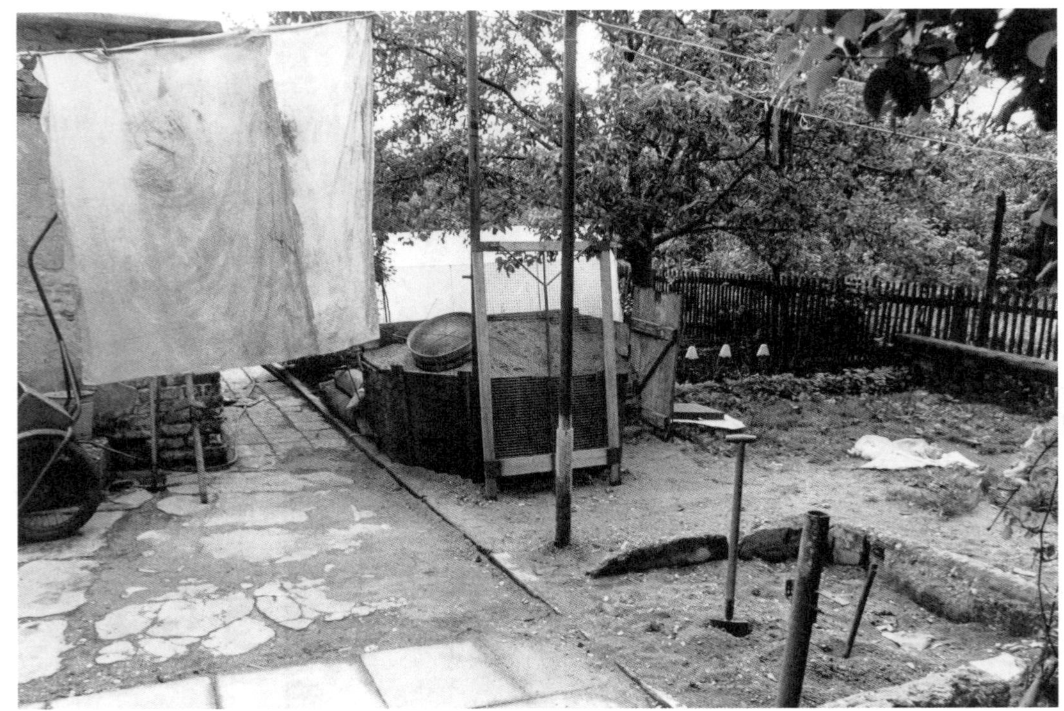

Regarding the balloon that was found, I can state: On Sunday, November 21, 1965, I noticed, while clearing snow, quite a large plastic cover in a tree on the property of my neighbor, Mr Kurt Meyer. As I assumed that my neighbor had attached this cover to protect the tree, I paid no more attention to the matter. The tree in question is a large, old apple tree of the Gravensteiner variety, a very tasty variety, which ripens in late August. It was only while measures were being taken by the People's Police to secure it that I realized the cover was a balloon. I have read through this statement, it accurately records the words I used and correspond to the statements made by me.

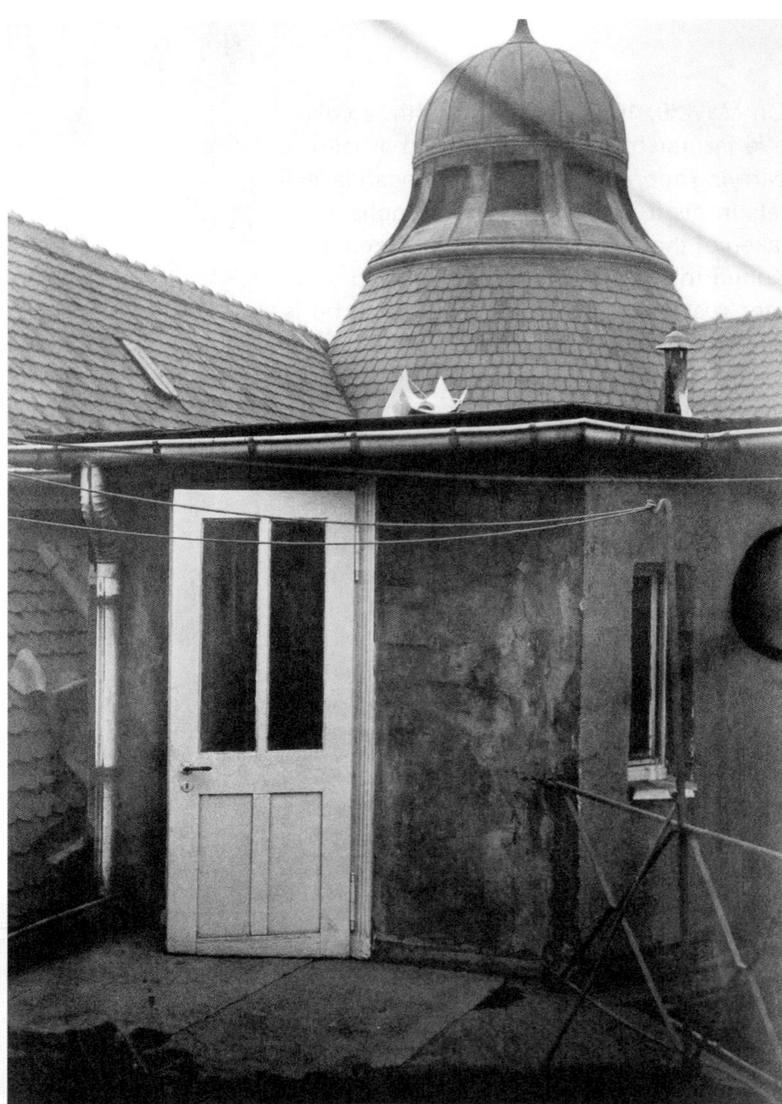

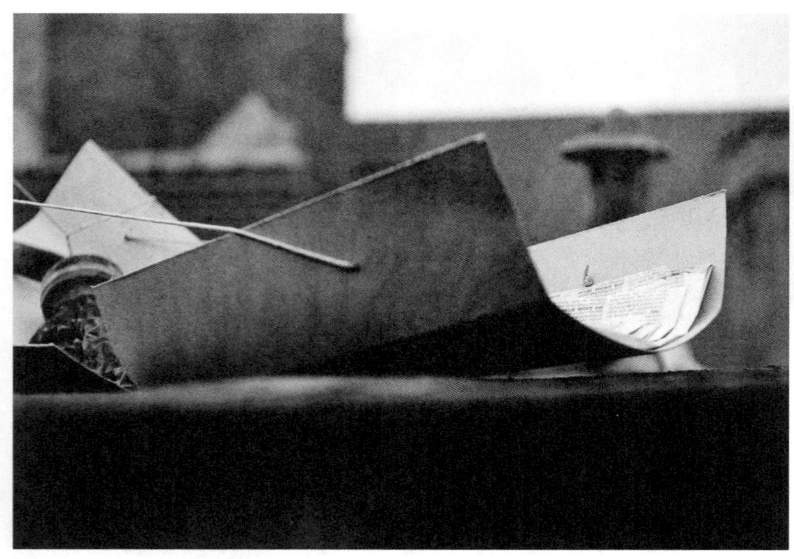

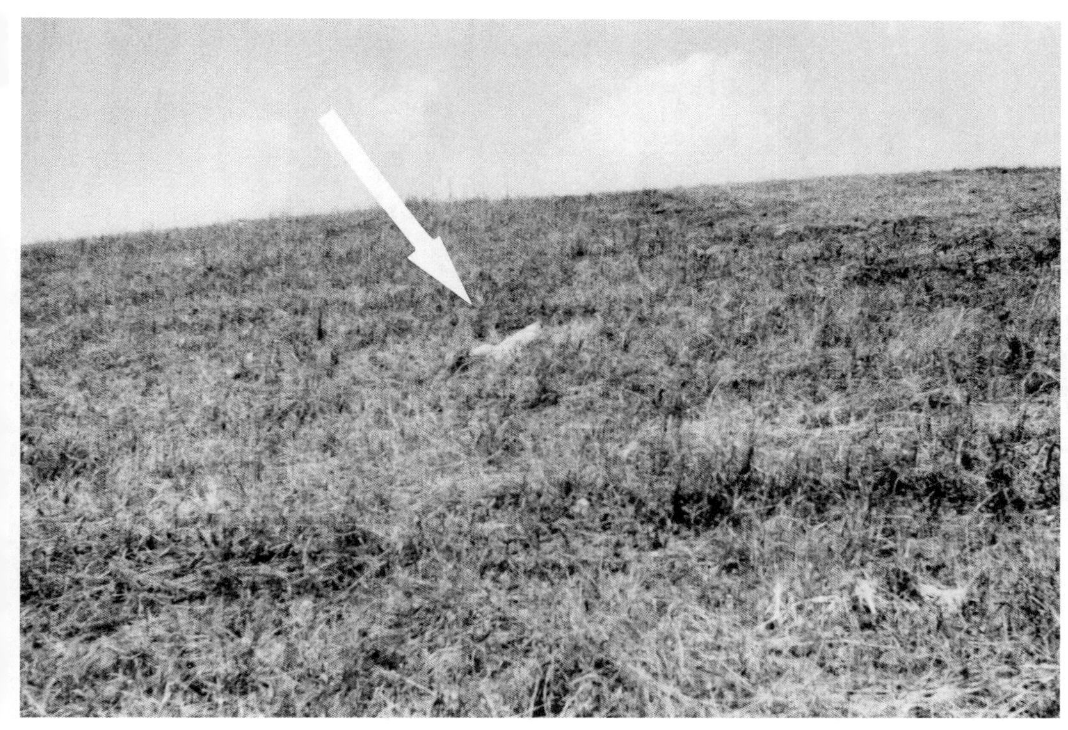

On March 26, 1966, at about 10:00 a. m., nineteen balloons that were sent up in the Helmstedt region came toward Magdeburg. One of the balloons burst over the town of Sommersdorf. The unopened package of propaganda leaflets fell onto the house of Mrs Linna Wünscher, a pensioner. The impact of the leaflets hitting the roof of the dwelling destroyed five roof tiles. Because it began to rain, new tiles were put on by neighbors so that it was not possible later to photograph the damage caused. The neighbors were unwilling to remove said tiles for a photo to prove what had happened. The leaflets did not get into the hands of the public.

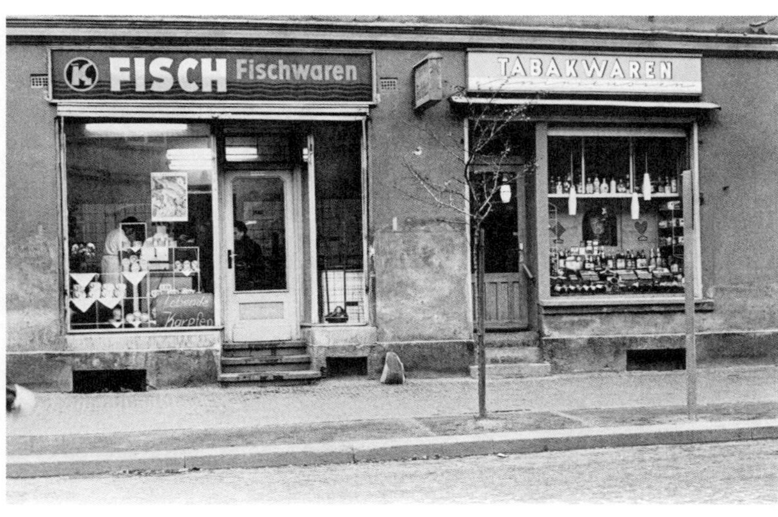

On September 29, 1966 at about 7 a. m., premises of the Walter Ulbricht VEB Leuna Works. At said time a balloon carrying no propaganda leaflets floated past the east side of the waste dump level with the South Train Station.

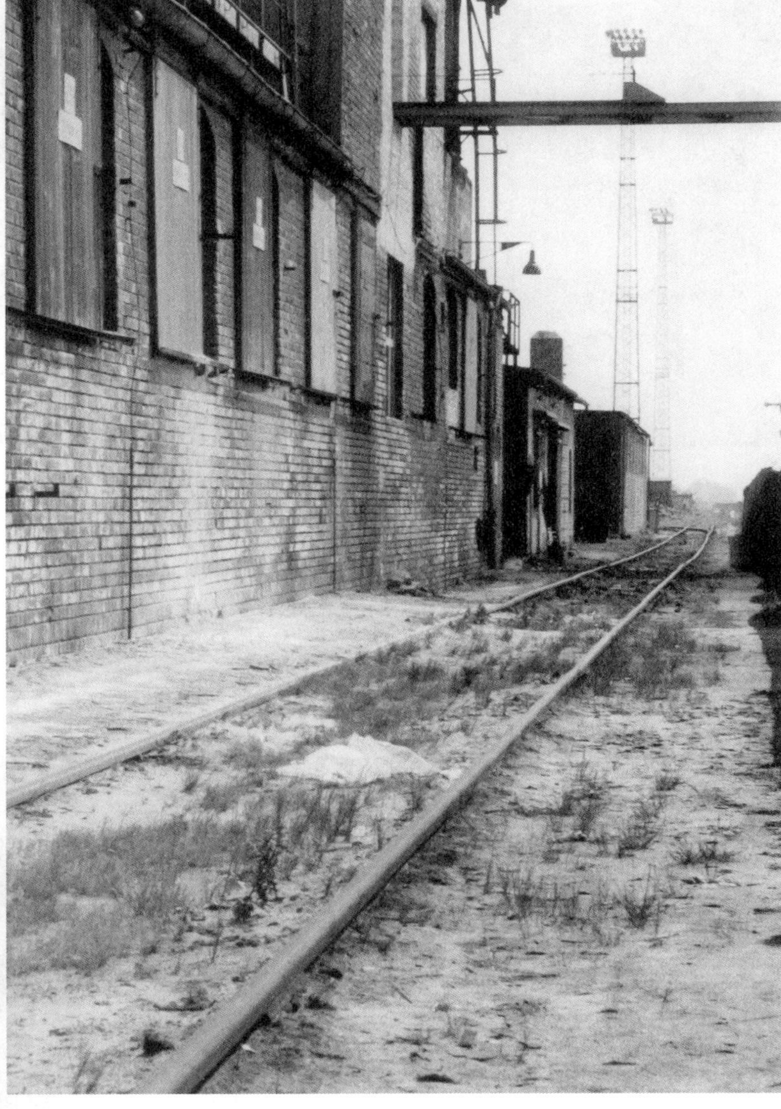

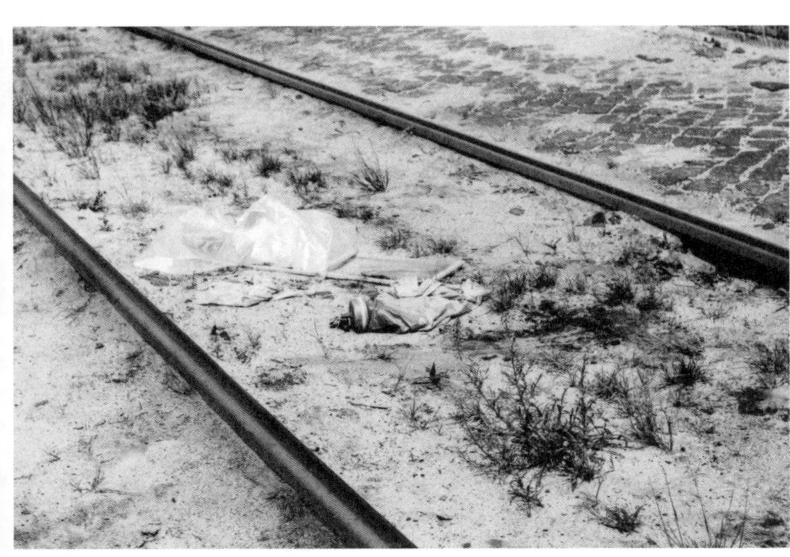

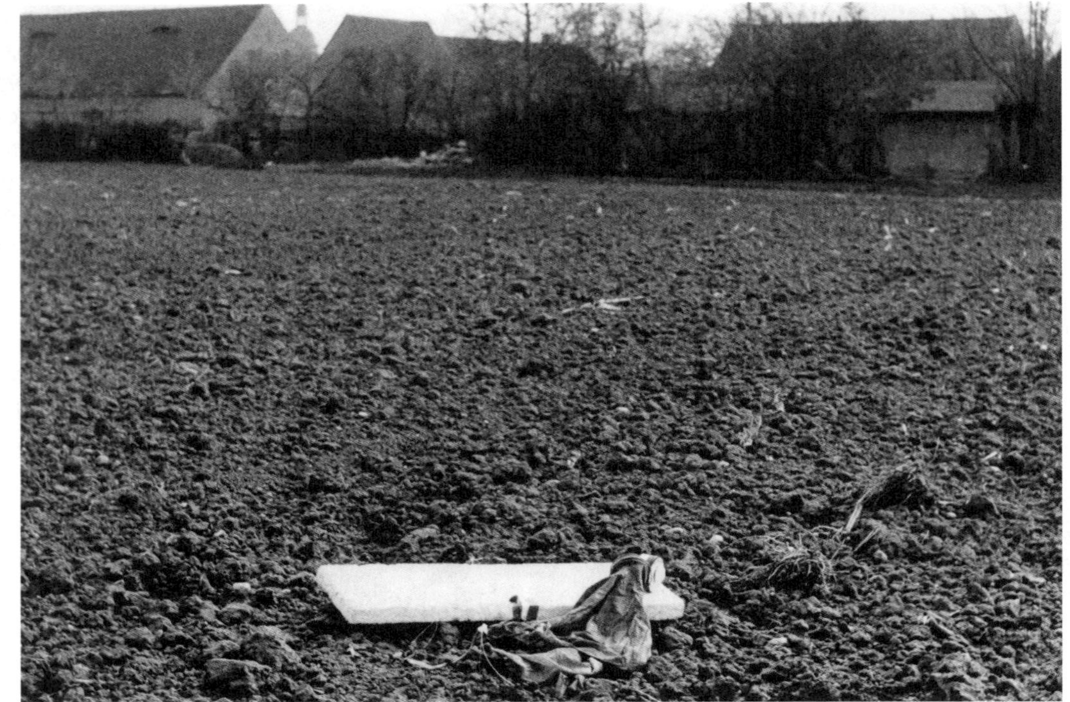

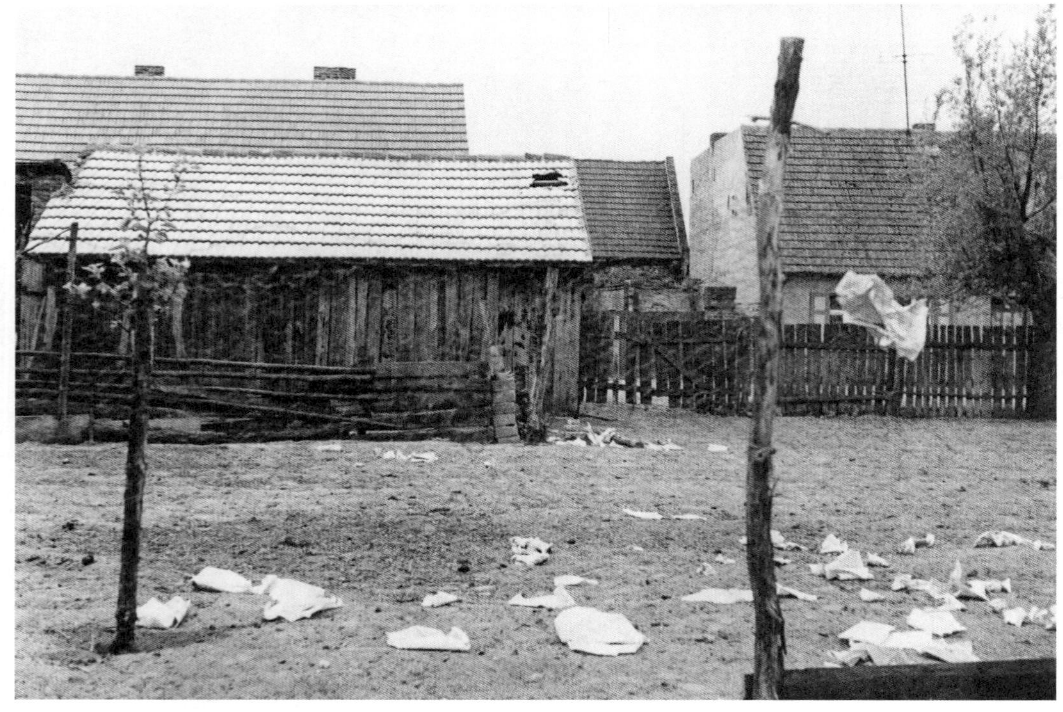

On May 23, 1966, at about 10 p.m., a large balloon carrying propaganda pamphlets exploded over Marktplatz in Quedlinburg, Halle District, at an altitude of twenty meters and emitted a large flame (three to five meters). No damage was incurred by persons or property. The find consisted of 500 copies of *Der Tag* No. 2 / May 1966.

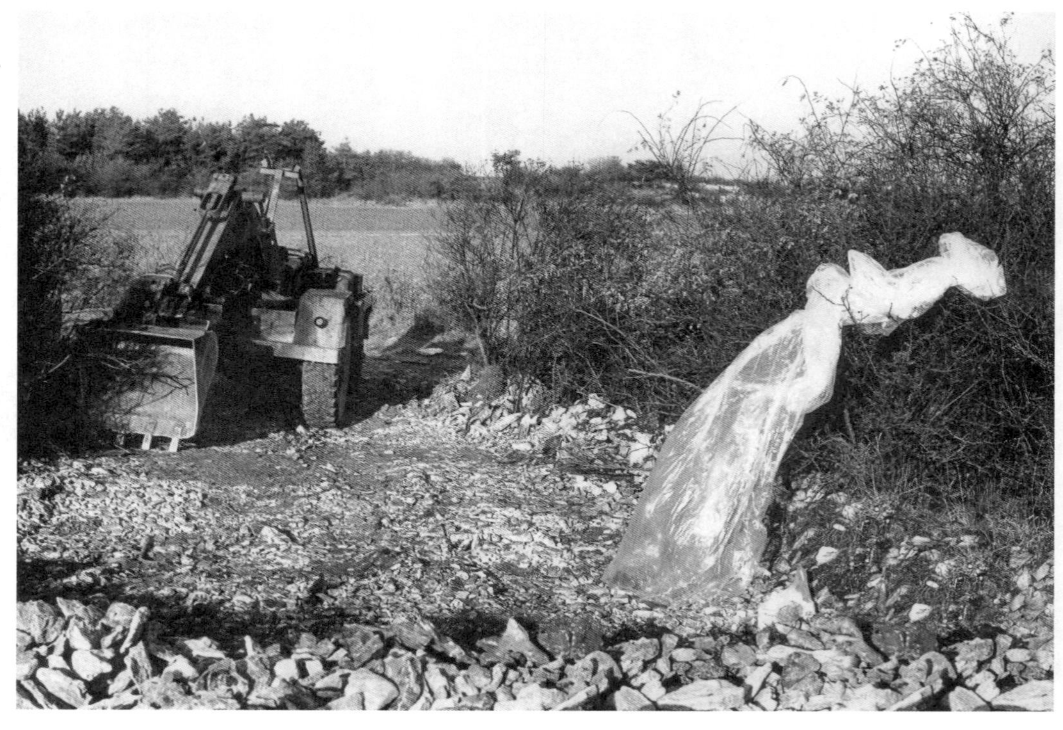

During the night of June 14, 1966 at about 1 a.m., Mrs Wiesner heard a noise with a squelching sound coming from her balcony. Assuming her husband's rubber boots had fallen to the ground, she attached no further significance to the noise. On June 15 at about 7 a.m. she stepped onto the balcony and discovered a collapsed balloon. Without touching it, she informed Mrs Gonschorekt, who lives in the building, and showed it to her. Neither woman had any idea of the use to which it had been put. Both persons are regarded as positive and discreet.

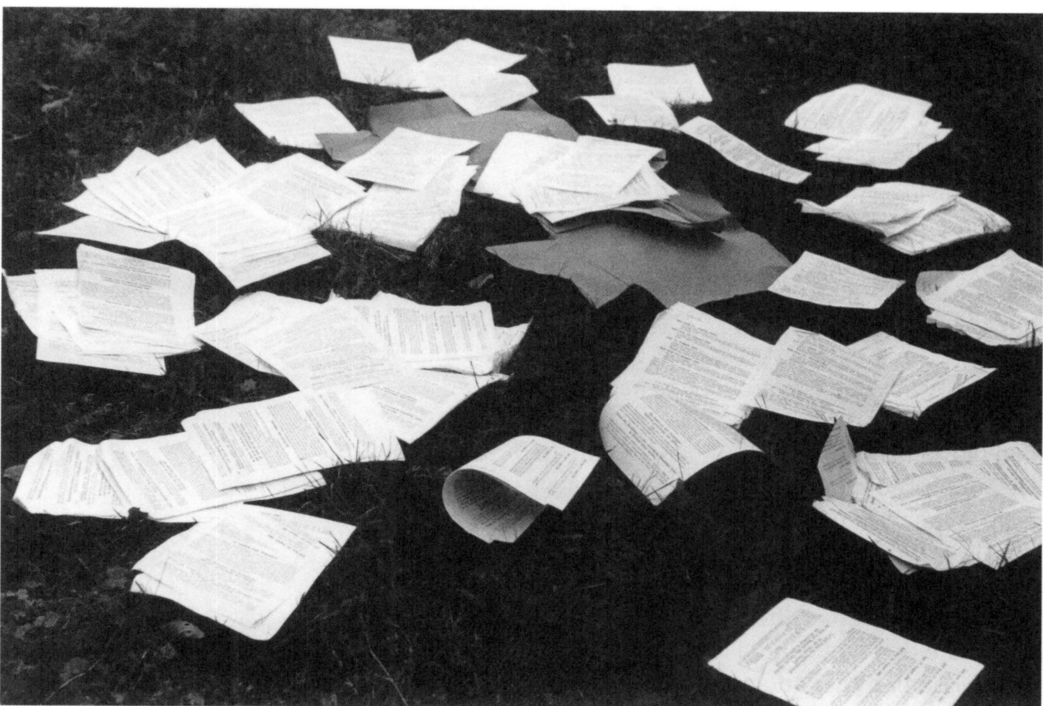

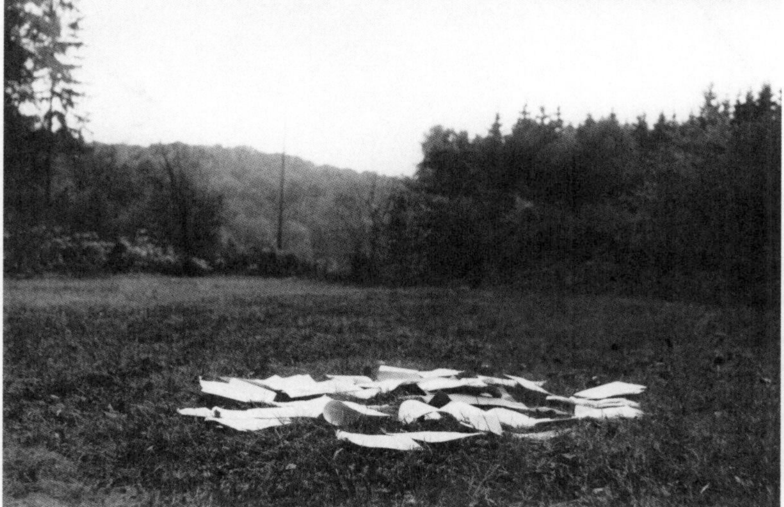

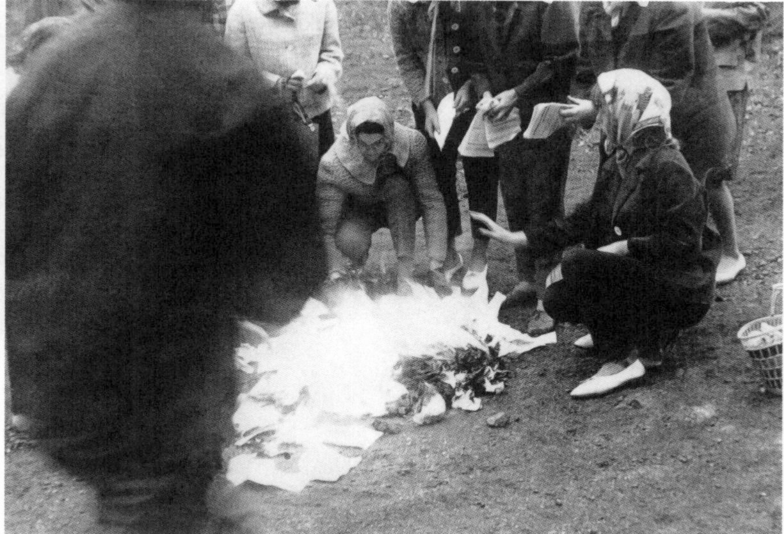

On August 8, 1966 half a hectare of forestry plantation land burned in Zossen District between the towns of Spremberg and Neuhof, between the Klausdorf intersection and the Forestry ranger's lodge. Shortly before twelve, balloons carrying propaganda leaflets were sighted in the area, seven of which exploded and burned in flight.

Between February 1968 and December 1968, 13,500 copies of *Flucht über See* (Flight Overseas) by Heinz R. Ockler, hardback, format 10 × 15 cm, were secured.

On May 19, 1967 around 2 p.m. a package of books, *Der lange Marsch* (The Long March), fell to the ground in Stendal. It broke through the greenhouse of the local market garden. A statement from the proprietor, a member of the NDPD, was waived because of his petty bourgeois attitude.

Klötze Region, Magdeburg District, July 1967. A balloon crashed through the roof of a garage on the LPG unit technical base. A balloon ripped off roof tiles and the gutter of a dwelling before going down in the garden. A balloon crashed through the roof of a dwelling and landed in the attic.

On March 31, 1966 Comrade Becker, a brick burner living in Hagenow, found a stack of *Information Berlin-Edition* propaganda leaflets in the corridor of the decommissioned kiln house at Brickworks II. He was at a loss to explain how those papers arrived at the site because the door was locked before he entered. While looking around, he happened to glance up, and saw a hole in the ceiling and the remains of a balloon hanging down. He concluded that the stack of leaflets must have fallen through the tile roof. Mrs Becker, who lives with her husband on the premises, said that she had heard something strike the roof on March 30 at about 10:45 p.m., after which the dog had barked loudly. She, however, assumed that adolescents were hanging around the kiln house again and attached no further significance to the incident. The recreation of the scene by the XX Division of the Schwerin Regional Office and the evidence secured in photographs showed that the balloon, which had flown in from the west at an altitude of 300 meters, had knocked a hole of about one square meter in the tile roof. The propaganda leaflets it carried weighed approximately fifteen kilograms.

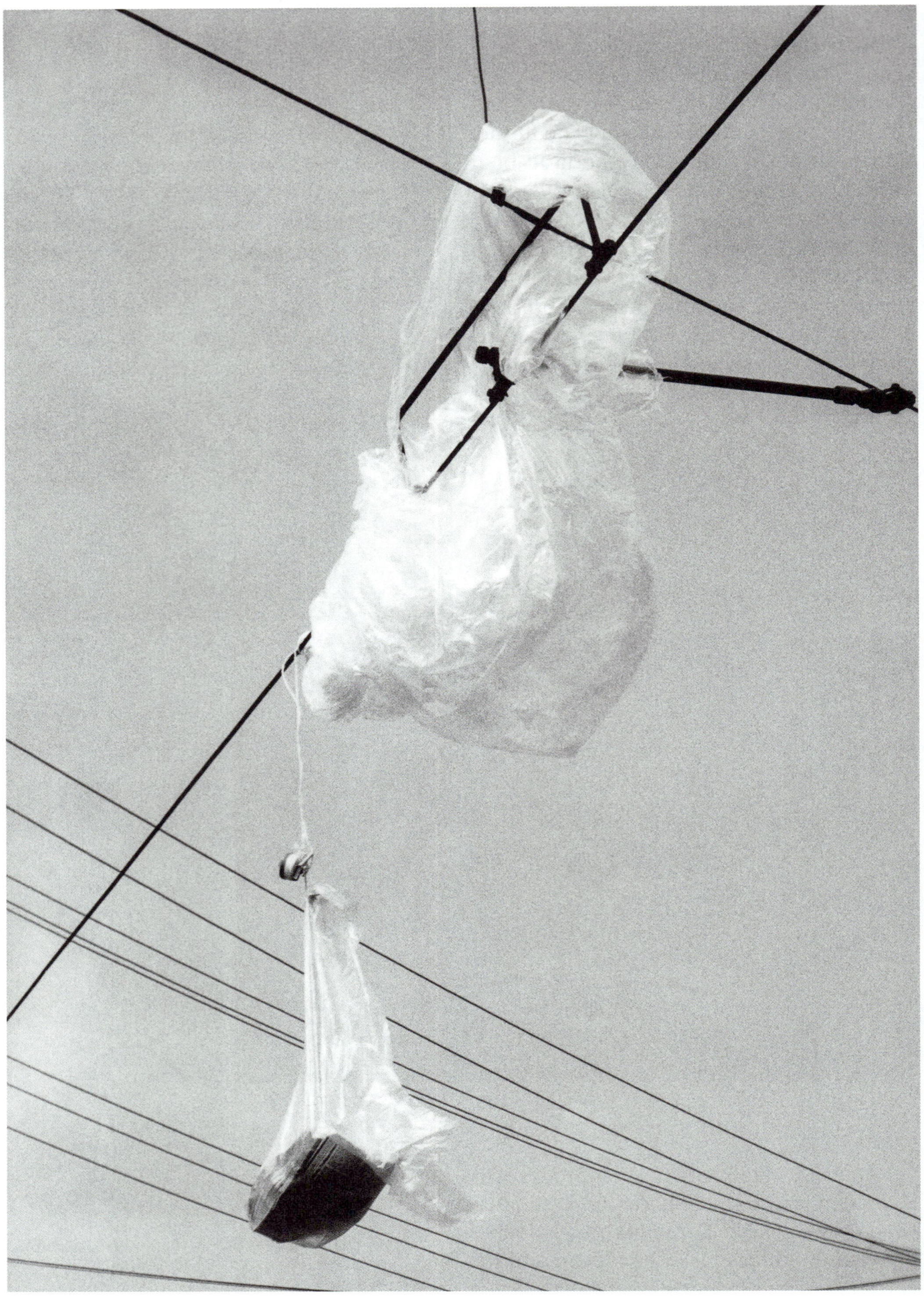

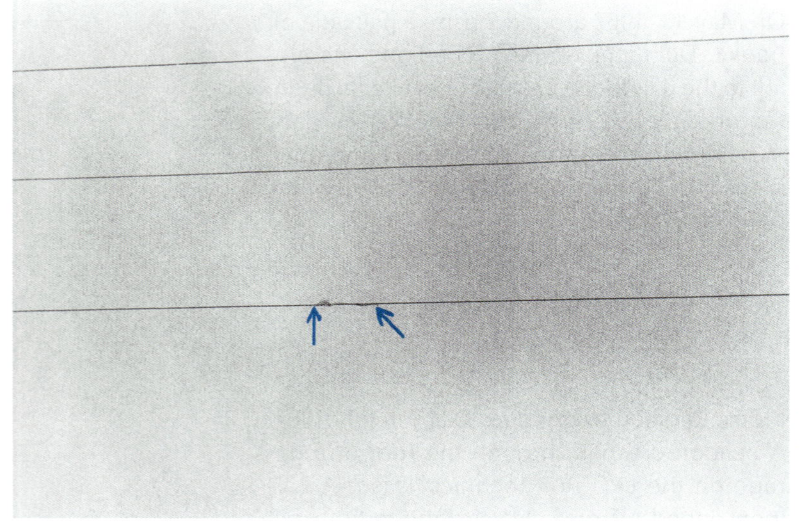

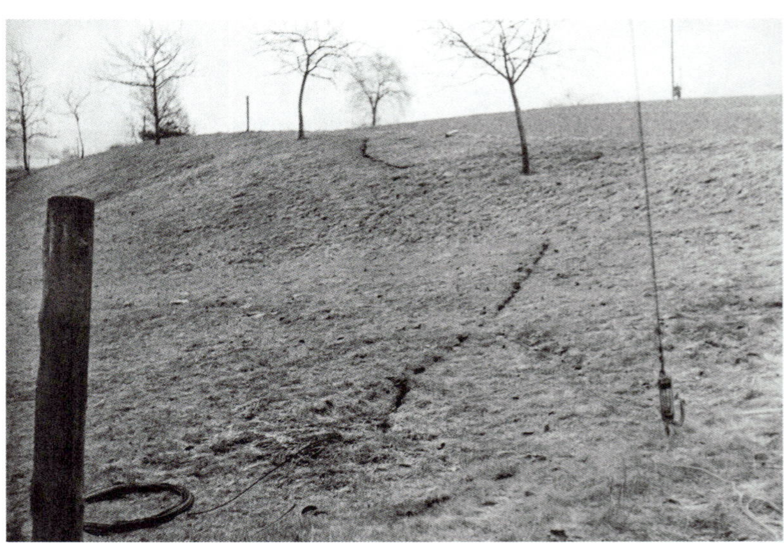

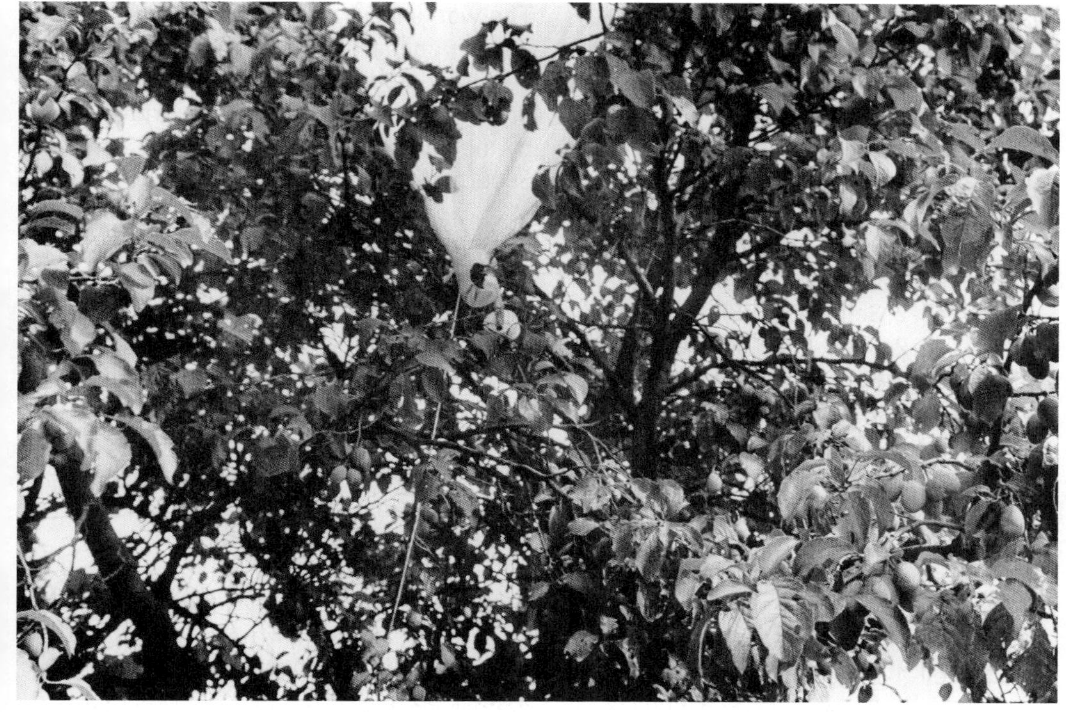

Eisenhüttenstadt, March 12, 1967, 1:15 a.m. Kurt Denner, together with his colleague Schmidtke and Comrade Thomas, were at the above-mentioned time loading ore in the EKO with his grab bucket crane. Toward 1:15 a.m., when Schmidtke was standing in front of his grab bucket crane, he saw that a balloon about two meters in diameter was hanging on a support pillar of the ore deposit catwalk, at the transition point from belt eight to belt nine. He called to his colleague about this discovery. At that moment the balloon was torn loose from the support pillar and was borne eastward by the wind. Comrade Thomas ran after the balloon, reaching it after 200 meters but could not hold onto it because of its volume. He desperately wanted to prevent the balloon from drifting on to the works grounds out of control. Only when Schmidtke, who was somewhat more sturdily built, and Denner, who was somewhat older, joined him, did all three working men succeeded in grabbing the balloon. The colleagues are of the opinion the balloon came in from a westerly direction, somewhere between the 300,000 cubic-meter, dry-seal gas holder and the pig casting machine above the slag heaps and then landed behind the slag heaps during a dead calm. There are no clues as to where it came from, except for the clock fastened to the balloon, which was still going at 2 a.m. and bore the stamp "Made in Germany."

In the night from January 31 to February 1st 1972 a balloon carrying about 5,000 propaganda pamphlets crashed through the roof and intermediate ceiling of a barn in Schwiesau. The barn is situated at the southern exit of the town in the direction of Berge. The exact time of the descent could not be ascertained. A hole measuring forty by fifty centimeters was caused in the roof, which is covered with corrugated asbestos roofing sheets, and one measuring fifty by one hundred centimeters in the intermediate ceiling. There were eighty dairy cows in the barn. None of the farm residents or animals incurred any injuries. Fright presumably caused a cow to calve prematurely. The healthy calf was given the name "Sputnik."

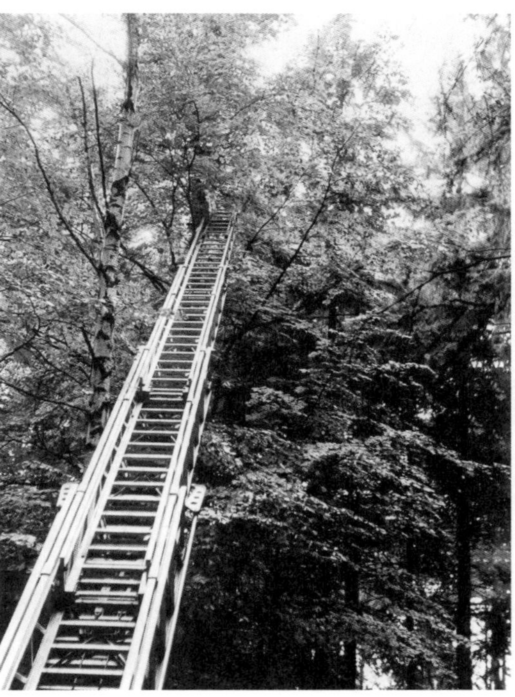

Jens Klein
Balloons

Graphic Design: Helmut Völter
Translation: Sarah Trenker
Proofreading: Sophia Holland
Lithography: Anders Forsmark
Typeface: Maxima
Printing: Druckhaus Sportflieger GmbH

Published by:
Spector Books
Harkortstraße 10
04107 Leipzig
www.spectorbooks.com

Distribution:
Germany, Austria: GVA, Gemeinsame Verlagsauslieferung Göttingen GmbH & Co. KG, www.gva-verlage.de; Switzerland: AVA Verlagsauslieferung AG, www.ava.ch; France, Belgium: Interart Paris, www.interart.fr; UK: Central Books Ltd, www.centralbooks.com; USA, Canada, Central and South America, Africa: Artbook / D.A.P., www.artbook.com; South Korea: The Book Society, www.thebooksociety.org; Japan: twelvebooks, www.twelve-books.com; Australia, New Zealand: Perimeter Distribution, www.perimeterdistribution.com

Supported by:
KUNSTMUSEUM MAGDEBURG KLOSTER UNSER LIEBEN FRAUEN KMd

First Edition: 2024
ISBN 978-3-95905-577-2

For Huschke

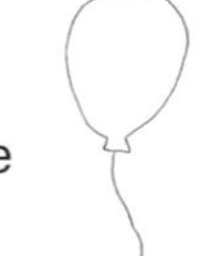

Image index
MfS-HA-XX-AKG- ...
... 5612-Teil-2-von-2-Seite-0184-Bild-0001
... 5612-Teil-1-Seite-0024
... 5612-Teil-1-von-2-Seite-0032-Bild-0001
... 5611-Teil-2-Seite-0125-Bild-0006
... 5612-Teil-2-von-2-Seite-0154-Bild-0002
... 5611-Teil-2-von-2-Seite-0160-Bild-0001
... 5612-Teil-1-von-2-Seite-0026-Bild-0001
... 5611-Teil-2-Seite-0095-Bild-0018A
... 5611-Teil-2-Seite-0095-Bild-0019A
... 5611-Teil-2-Seite-0095-Bild-0020A
... 5611-Teil-2-von-2-Seite-0125-Bild-0005
... 5611-Teil-2-Seite-0180-Bild-0002
... 5611-Teil-2-von-2-Seite-0125-Bild-0009
... 5612-Teil-1-Seite-0052-Bild-0002
... 5612-Teil-1-Seite-0051-Bild-0002
... 5612-Teil-1-Seite-0052-Bild-0001
... 5611-Teil-2-Seite-0125-Bild-0002
... 5612-Teil-1-Seite-0027-Bild-0001
... 5611-Teil-1-Seite-0032-Bild-0002
... 5611-Teil-1-Seite-0032-Bild-0003
... 5611-Teil-1-Seite-0033-Bild-0001
... 5612-Teil-1-Seite-0033-Bild-0001
... 5611-Teil-2-Seite-0093
... 5611-Teil-2-Seite-0095-Bild-0015A
... 5611-Teil-2-Seite-0125-Bild-0007
... 5611-Teil-2-Seite-0089-Bild-0002
... 5611-Teil-2-Seite-0091-Bild-0003
... 5612-Teil-1-Seite-0039
... 5612-Teil-2-Seite-0137-Bild-0003
... 5611-Teil-2-Seite-0119-Bild-0073
... 5611-Teil-2-Seite-0170-Bild-0001
... 5611-Teil-1-Seite-0038-Bild-0002
... 5612-Teil-1-Seite-0036-Bild-0001
... 5611-Teil-2-Seite-0176
... 5611-Teil-2-Seite-0175-Bild-0002
... 5611-Teil-2-Seite-0091-Bild-0001
... 5611-Teil-1-Seite-0045-Bild-0001
... 5611-Teil-1-Seite-0045-Bild-0002
... 5611-Teil-2-Seite-0088
... 5611-Teil-1-von-2-Seite-0022-Bild-0009
... 5611-Teil-1-Seite-0042-Bild-0002
... 5611-Teil-1-Seite-0042-Bild-0005
... 5612-Teil-1-Seite-0117-Bild-0001
... 5611-Teil-2-Seite-0173-Bild-0001
... 5612-Teil-2-Seite-0141-Bild-0007
... 5612-Teil-2-Seite-0192-Bild-0002
... 5612-Teil-2-Seite-0194-Bild-0002
... 5612-Teil-2-Seite-0202-Bild-0002
... 5611-Teil-2-Seite-0178
... 5612-Teil-1-Seite-0022-Bild-0002
... 5611-Teil-2-Seite-0189-Bild-0001
... 5611-Teil-2-Seite-0094-Bild-0001
... 5612-Teil-1-Seite-0012-Bild-0001
... 5612-Teil-1-Seite-0010-Bild-0001

The works illustrated are based on photographs from the Federal Archives, taken and compiled by the State Security of the GDR. These texts were written by the author and are inspired by State Security files.

MfS: Ministerium für Staatssicherheit (Ministry for State Security)
HA XX: Hauptabteilung XX (Main Department XX)
AKG: Auswertungs- und Kontrollgruppe (Evaluation and Control Group)

DDR: Deutsche Demokratische Republik (German Democratic Republic)
EKO: Eisenhüttenkombinat Ost (Steelworks Combinate East)
DGB: Deutscher Gewerkschaftsbund (Federation of German Trade Unions)
LPG: Landwirtschaftliche Produktionsgenossenschaft (Agricultural Production Cooperative)
VEB: Volkseigener Betrieb (Publicly Owned Enterprise, the main legal form of companies in the former GDR)
NDPD: National-Demokratische Partei Deutschlands (National Democratic Party of Germany)